S0-ADL-212

The Handbook of Dog Breeds

The Handbook of Dog Breeds

Maria Costantino

**BARNES
&NOBLE
BOOKS**
NEW YORK

This edition published by Barnes & Noble, Inc.,
By arrangement with D&S Books Ltd

2004 Barnes & Noble Books

M   10   9   8   7   6   5   4   3   2   1

ISBN 0-7607-5657-0

All rights reserved. No part of this publication may be reproduced,
stored in a retrieval system, or transmitted in any way or by any means,
electronic, mechanical, photocopying, recording or otherwise, without
the prior written permission of the copyright holder.

Creative Director: Sarah King
Editor: Clare Haworth-Maden
Project Editor: Judith Millidge
Photographer: Paul Forrester
Designer: Axis Design

Map Images © Cadmium Systems
Picture p242 © The Kennel Club Picture Library

© 2003 D&S Books Ltd

D&S Books Ltd
Kerswell, Parkham Ash,
Bideford, Devon, EX39 5PR

Printed in China

Contents

Introduction

"Plus on apprend à connaitre l'homme,

plus on apprend à éstimer le chien"

(The more one gets to know of men,

the more one values dogs)

"L'Esprit des bêtes" 1847, by A. Toussenel (1803-85)

THE WOLF: THE DOMESTICATED DOG'S CLOSE RELATIVE.

From Wolf Pack to Canine Companion: the Evolution of the Dog

The ancestors of today's dogs appear to have been the now extinct family of carnivorous mammals called miacis, which evolved sometime around 50 million years ago. Many authorities believe, however, that the extinct hesperocyon, a carnivore which evolved between 38 and 26 million years ago in what is now North America, is, in fact, the dog's most distant ancestor. Fossil remains show that this ancient species had an inner ear anatomy that is characteristic of the canine family. Meanwhile, a second carnivorous group was evolving: the tomarctus, an animal with a long body and tail, and social instincts similar to those of the dog, dominated Eurasia, and for a while was thought to be the dog's ancestor. Recent research however, has questioned this, and it is now believed that the tomarctus died out, leaving the hesperocyon to develop evolve as a canine, *Canis davisi*, some 10 million years ago. This canine is believed to have migrated across the Bering land bridge, spreading throughout Asia, Europe, and Africa and, during the next eight million years, diverged into the Canidae, the ancestors of the modern canine.

7

These ancient canines shared many of the characteristics still visible in modern canines such as wolves: long skulls, semi-rigid and sturdy hind legs, and supple, loose front legs, which are attached to the body only by muscles. Like the wolf, they also had thick, insulating fur, small feet and large teeth for catching, holding, and tearing prey. These were all combined with a very large brain, excellent hearing, and exceptional scenting skills. These mammals may have been solitary hunters at one time, but as climate changes occurred – around two million years ago, tropical forests gave way to open grasslands and steppes – the carnivorous canines' prey, the herbivores, became herd animals.

These early canines either had, or developed very soon, a social structure, that allowed them to hunt in packs so they could now bring down and kill animals much larger than themselves. It was this canine ability to form social relationships that was the basis for its success as a species.

The domestic dog is a member of the genus *Canis*, which also includes wolves, jackals, and coyote – the dog's closest relatives – as well as the more distant relatives, foxes (all 21 species), the African wild dog, the maned wolf of Central and South America, the dhole of India, the bush dog of Africa, and the racoon dog of the far-eastern regions of Asia. All share a common ancestral past and a large range of similar behaviors.

It is now generally agreed that an early form of the Asiatic wolf, *Canis lupus pallipes*, was the first canine to form a relationship with humans, since wolves, unlike coyote and jackals, are far more social in their behavior. No one quite knows when this relationship began because the earliest evidence dating from around 12,000 BC suggests that the canine was already a dog, and not a semi-tamed wolf that was coexisting with man.

WOLF CUBS, LIKE PUPPIES, LEARN FROM THEIR MOTHERS.

The domestication of animals seems to have been a continual process since, in some parts of the world, early man – the hunter-gatherer – was still trying to 'subdue' or domesticate primitive dogs, while in other parts, man had settled in lands to become the first farmers, which allowed them to begin the process of selective breeding in order to produce dogs employed to herd and guard their livestock.

There are many theories given for the domestication of the wolf-dog. The most common is that at the time the first wolf-dogs were being domesticated, man was a primitive hunter-gatherer. The beautiful prehistoric rock paintings from Altamira in Spain, show dog-like figures accompanying hunters on the trail of herd animals like deer and bison.

Wolves were widespread throughout Europe, Asia and North America and, until their numbers were hugely restricted by man, wolves were the most widespread of all land mammals. They were undoubtedly hunted by early man as food, and possibly kept as a food reserve during lean times. Evidence from Colima state in Mexico suggests that the Mexican hairless dog was bred specifically for food. Even in more recent history, dogs have been eaten during times of starvation, as in the siege of Leningrad and during the occupation of the Channel Islands during World War II. Earlier in the 19th century, during the siege of Paris when the city was blockaded and its citizens starving, dogs and cats were eaten and, it is said, to disguise the origins of their meat, French chefs devised the many ingenious sauces and cooking techniques that eventually became the basis of *haute cuisine*. In Mongolia and Manchuria, China, the chow-chow was once not only a useful dog for guarding and cart-pulling, but its meat was considered a delicacy and its fur popular for clothing.

THE CHOW-CHOW: ONE-TIME GUARD DOG, DRAFT ANIMAL AND A GASTRONOMIC DELICACY.

It is possible that, after killing a nursing bitch for food, the wolf pups were taken 'home' by the hunters and then became socialized into the human family group. Although the pups were tamed, they remained wolves, with an instinctive love of hunting. Now both human and wolf were hunting the same prey together and both used the same techniques: panicking the herds and isolating the old or injured animals that were easier to kill. While humans had the advantage of hands for making and holding tools and weapons for killing, wolves had the advantage of scent and speed. If man or wolf pack made a killing, it was of interest to the other, since both were scavengers.

As man improved his hunting skills and weaponry, wolves would more often become the followers of the hunting parties as these were more likely to produce rich results with least effort. Now wolves would hang around the camp sites, scavenging for scraps and being 'rewarded' for providing an early warning of the presence of intruders or predators.

A second theory assumes that the wolf became domesticated because of man's garbage! The cast-off bones on the dump of the campsite were tempting tidbits and

DOGS WERE OFTEN TRAINED AS DRAFT ANIMALS.

wolves could be encouraged by man to become friendly through rewards. Once dogs became used to humans, they not only kept the campsites clean, but also jealously guarded their new companions. For some time this theory was given little credence, but more recently, observations made of still-primitive tribes in New Guinea have demonstrated that those tribes without dogs have to move their village sites frequently as their garbage dumps grow in size. Those tribes which had scavenging dogs, however, have more permanently settled villages.

A third theory suggests that dogs were domesticated to serve man as beasts of burden – to pull a travois or sledge. A travois consists of two trailing poles fastened into a dog's harness. The poles are held apart and parallel by webbing and on this a load is lashed. Dogs may have pulled a travois in summer and a sledge across the winter snow. In northern Europe, deposits of a sledge dating from around 6000 BC so support this theory. Although it is not known when the first human migrants reached the Arctic, they could not have done so without domestic dogs for both transport and food. Lost and starving Inuit – and European explorers – have been known to eat their dogs: this desperate act of eating their transport, in fact, often made their own deaths more certain.

CANINE IMAGERY APPEARS IN MANY ANCIENT CULTURES.

Whatever theory is subscribed to, and despite the fact that the dog was probably the first animal to be domesticated, the process was slow. As man domesticated other animals, dogs had to learn not to kill them but herd and protect them and, as man spread himself across the entire world, dogs had to adapt to their new terrain and climates as well.

This process of adaptation continues today as dogs learn to live in a huge variety of circumstances and situations: as working dogs on farms and hunts, as police, rescue, and guard dogs, as guide and hearing dogs assisting their owners, as pets in high-rise apartments in cities or on the road with their migrant owners- whether 'travellers' or long-distance truck drivers, or even like Leica, in a spacecraft!

RATHER THAN PULLING LOADS, MOST MODERN DOGS ARE THEMSELVES CARRIED!

THE COLOSSEUM IN ROME: THE GREAT 'CIRCUS' OR ARENA WHERE COMBAT BETWEEN DOGS WAS A REGULAR SPECTACLE.

While natural environmental pressures resulted in the wolf becoming relaxed around humans, it was only after several generations of selective breeding by humans that the great diversity of dog breeds developed. Pictures from ancient Egyptian tombs indicate that by around 2000 BC there were already elaborately spotted dogs, dogs with short legs, dogs with erect ears, dogs with drooping or pendulous ears like greyhounds, and dogs with tightly curled tails. These images point to the fact that the Egyptians were among the first cultures to breed and employ dogs for specific purposes. The gaze hound, a dog which hunts by sight, and which, by sheer speed is able to run down its quarry, originated in the North Africa where the clear light gave good visibility, but the dry air of the desert made for poor scenting. The Egyptian god Anubis, whose responsibility it was to escort the souls of the dead to their final judgement was depicted in art with the body of a man and the head of a dog, or more properly, a jackal. Although the Greek historian Herodotus wrote that Egyptians mourned when dogs died, they never were held in as high esteem as cats: thousands of mummified cats were discovered at Bubastis, the cult centre for the worship of the cat-god Bast, while the mummified remains of dogs are rare.

Like the ancient Greeks, the Romans also used dogs in their religious ceremonies, as sacrificial animals: in Greece a kennel was maintained at the sanctuary of Asclepius, the god of healing, at Epidaurus. Although Asclepius is more usually depicted with a staff and sacred snake, sometimes he was shown with a dog which was reputed to heal the sick

with his lick! In both cultures, while using dogs as sacrificial animals was probably a good way of controlling the canine population, they were, nonetheless, held in high regard and with affection as both Greek and Roman folk tales abound with stories of a dog's fearlessness and fidelity – from which word we derive the name 'Fido'. Dog-shaped household objects such as oil lamps and purely decorative figures of dogs were popular in Roman homes throughout the empire and the very Roman tradition of an image of a dog inscribed with the words *'cave canem'* or 'beware of the dog', persists today!

Further east, in Mesopotamia – the ancient lands lying between the rivers Euphrates and Tigris in Asia Minor – was the home of the

WHILE ISLAM REGARDED CATS AS 'BLESSED', DOGS WERE UNCLEAN ANIMALS.

Abyssinian, and later, the Babylonian Empires. The British Museum in London houses a magnificent collection of bas reliefs dating from around 645 BC from the city of Nineveh and showing the Assyrian king Ashurbanipal hunting with great mastiff-type dogs. Such dogs became famed for their fearlessness and were bred by the Romans for hunting and battle, as well as for use in gladiatorial combat – against both men and other dogs.

NEAPOLITAN MASTIFF

13

THE CHINESE CREATED MINIATURE DOGS AS COMPANIONS.

In contrast, written records in China dating back some 4,000 years reveal that the 'fu' or 'lion dog', a recurring theme in Chinese culture, was regarded as 'lucky' and brought both great happiness and good fortune. It also seems that China was responsible for both dwarfing and miniaturisation of breeds to create companion dogs, as well as breeding the first pack hunting dogs.

Some 2,750 years ago in Persia, (now modern Iran) the religion Zoroastrianism was introduced and in the *Zend Avesta*, the scared books of the religion, one volume is devoted to the care and breeding of dogs. When, later, Islam became the major religious belief, cats were 'blessed' animals, while dogs were regarded as 'unclean'. This is probably because Islam requires strict observance of hygiene and sanitation, and in a region where rabies was, and is still, a problem, the need to 'cleanse' after being in contact with dogs was a most sensible precaution.

Throughout history, invading armies took their fighting dogs with them and brought home, on their return, the dogs of those they conquered. In the Middle Ages, as European trade routes became more widespread, different types of dog began to spread across the known world and the medieval practices of hunting led to the development of more varieties of dog, such as scent and sight hounds, bred specifically for this purpose. In the 1300s, the first books on sports hunting, a 'pastime' of the rich and noble classes were written: in France, Guillaume Twici wrote *Le Art de*

Venerie, while in Spain, the King Alfonso XI of Castile and Leon himself wrote *Libro de Monteria*. The first English text, *The Master of Game*, in which hunting dogs were discussed, was produced later in the early 1400s by Edward, Duke of York. But it wasn't until the late 16th century that the first attempts to 'classify' dogs was made by Dr. John Caius in his *De Canibus Britannicis*. Technology has also played its part in the development of dog breeds: with the introduction of the gun, new breeds of dogs which could 'set', 'point', 'flush' and retrieve shot game were required. Dogs bred for these purposes first appeared on the Iberian Peninsula (Spain and Portugal) and spread from there throughout Europe.

Today there are more than 400 recognized breeds and breed varieties throughout the world: many new breeds will be created, and some breeds will become extinct as man continues to develop and 'alter' the dog to fit in with modern needs or to suit his preference for a certain physical feature or temperament. In the show rings, these contemporary fashions in canine appearance are on display, and there still remain those dogs which are selected for their abilities rather than their looks, such as police and service dogs and working sheepdogs. However, there are also those dogs of crossbreed and indeterminate breed – the mongrels – whose appearance and utility skill are ultimately of less value in many peoples' lives than their role as faithful friend and companion. While today the dog breeds are categorized in part on their origins and physical characteristics, and in part on their behavior characteristics, these categories are largely arbitrary: every dog, regardless of appearance or behavior, ultimately shares a very long 'pedigree' indeed.

'POINTING' DOGS WERE BRED IN RESPONSE TO THE NEW TECHNOLOGY OFFERED TO FARMERS IN THE FORM OF GUNS.

Chapter 1

Anatomy & Senses

"I am his Highness' dog at Kew;

Pray, tell me sir, whose dog are you?"

Epigram Engraved on the Collar of a Dog which I gave to his Royal Highness, (1738)

Alexander Pope (1688-1744)

Anatomy of the Dog

Flews – pendulous upper lips, especially at the inner corners

Occiput – highest point of skull

Stop – indentation between the eyes where nasal bone and skull meet

Crest – upper arched portion of neck

Brisket – below chest, between front legs

Withers – highest point of body, behind neck

Hock – dog's true heel

Stifle – joint between upper and lower thighs

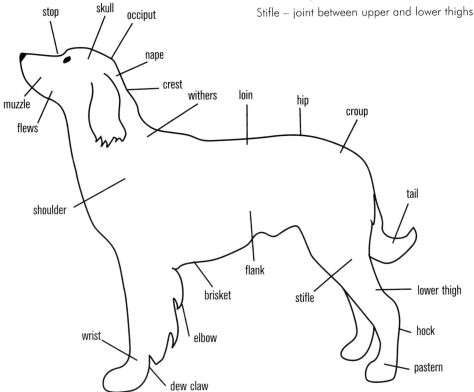

MINIATURE BREEDS: THE CHIHUAHUA FROM MEXICO.

however, keeps all of the skeletons 'normal' anatomical relationships, but reduces the size of the long limb bones and enlarges the joints. Breeds such as the basset hound and dachshund are examples of dwarfed breeds. Both miniaturisation and dwarfing are natural occurrences and, furthermore, they can both take place together, making it possible to have breeds such as miniature dachshunds!

In puppies, the long limb bones start as hollow tubes of cartilage and, only as the puppy grows are they replaced by bone. The outside of the 'tube', the periosteum, produces new bone cells and increases the thickness of the bone, while increases in the length of bones happens near the ends of the bones, at the epiphyseal plates, as areas of

Since living in the wild, dogs have evolved and adapted extraordinarily well to cope with the enormous range of conditions in which they live. Yet all dogs share the same basic – some might even say fairly primitive – skeleton, even though selective breeding has brought about numerous changes in their outward appearance.

The first dogs seem to have been about the size of the dingo, and were mature in their growth by about 10 months old. Around 5,000 years ago, selective breeding had produced the enhanced size of great mastiff dogs, while late selective breeding helped to diminish the size of some dogs. Miniaturization proportionally reduces the size of each bone – skull, ribs and limb bones – and resulted in breeds such as the Yorkshire terrier and Chihuahua. Dwarfing

THE MINIATURE DACHSHUND FROM GERMANY.

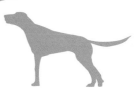

cartilage are converted to bone. The growth of the bones at the epiphyseal plates is regulated by hormone activity and, consequently, larger breeds of dogs, which need longer periods for their bones to grow, also reach sexual maturity later than smaller breeds, which need less time for their bone lengths to fix.

The bones are joined together at the cartilaginous joints and surrounded by a capsule containing a lubricating fluid, while ligaments anchor the bones to each other and allow movement in a specific direction and prevent excessive movement in other directions. Muscles are attached to these tendons. There are three types of muscle in dogs: skeletal, smooth and cardiac. Skeletal muscles can be controlled by the dog: they can be relaxed or contracted at will. An obvious example of this muscle control can be seen in the tail, which can be curled up, lowered, raised or wagged at will. Smooth muscle controls the movement of the viscera or 'entrails', while cardiac muscle makes up the bulk of a dog's heart.

LLASO APSO: ONE OF THE FOUR TIBETAN BREEDS, BRED AS A COMPANION TO BUDDHIST MONKS.

The terms used to describe a dog's head can be a little confusing at first: the head consists of the nose, then the muzzle, which extends to just before or between the eyes. This point is called the stop, which in some breeds can be dramatic, while in others, it appears to be absent. Then the skull begins and reaches its highest point at a crest known as the occiput.

There are also three basic skull shapes in dogs. The first is the dolichocephalus or long nose shape where the 'natural' skull shape of the wolf has been elongated. This skull shape is apparent in breeds such as borzois, Salukis and greyhounds. The second skull shape is called mesocephalic and describes the medium-sized skull that is evident on dogs such as pointers. The third skull type is the brachycephalic which describes the 'diminished' skull shape found in snub-nosed breeds such as boxers. In breeds such as pugs, the brachycephalic skull shape has been taken to the extreme and the muzzle has all but disappeared.

THE GERMAN LONG-HAIRED POINTER DISPLAYS THE MESOCEPHALIC SKULL SHAPE.

PUG: AN EXAMPLE OF A BRACHYCEPHALIC SKULL SHAPE.

BORZOI: AN EXAMPLE OF THE ELONGATED DOLICHOCEPHALIC SKULL SHAPE.

TEETH NEED CARE.

Doggie Dentition

The teeth of a dog are those of a carnivore, designed to bite, tear, cut, and grind. A normal dog has 42 teeth: 20 in the upper jaw and 22 in the lower. The six front teeth on the upper and lower jaw are the incisors, the biting teeth, which meet in a scissor-like action with the top incisors fitting neatly over the lower ones. As well as biting, these teeth are also used for nibbling and for grooming. Directly behind these are the canines, or 'tusks'. Each jaw has two canine teeth, with one on each side. These very strong teeth are designed to seize and hold prey and to tear off muscle and skin from bones and to tear out the internal organs of their prey. There are a further eight premolar teeth on each jaw and six molar teeth on the lower jaw, with four molars on the upper jaw. The premolars and molars are used as cutters and crushers. Because a dog's teeth are deeply set in the jaw and covered with very hard enamel, these molars and premolars are extremely hard and, when coupled with the strength of the jaw muscles, make it possible for dogs to crush bones. Saliva lubricates the food after it has been chewed, easing its entry into the digestive system.

Like humans, dogs grow first, or milk, teeth, which are then lost during the growing period. In puppies, the upper incisors are pushed out at about 14 weeks old, as the permanent teeth erupt. The lower incisors however are changed some weeks later, and the canines at about 18 weeks. Unlike humans, however, dogs rarely suffer from tooth cavities. Firstly, dogs don't consume large amounts of sugar and secondly, dogs' teeth are not so tightly packed in their mouths that food gets stuck between them. Furthermore, canine teeth are smoother than those of a human – there are fewer pits and fissures in the biting surfaces where food can collect and rot. Dogs can, however, suffer from periodontal disease, a bacterial disease of the tissue that surrounds and supports the teeth. This disease, though preventable with routine oral hygiene – regular brushing with an attractively flavored toothpaste – nevertheless affects some 70% of 'companion' dogs over four years old.

DOG TRAINING OVERRIDES THE LIMBIC SYSTEM.

AWARE OF TIME AND WHAT'S GOING ON.

Clever Canines

Dogs' brains are much smaller than human ones, especially the part of the brain known as the cerebrum. This part of the brain is associated with intellectual functions, emotions, and personalities. Instead, much of a dog's brain is concerned with sensory activities, such as sight, hearing and, especially scent. Dogs' brains store information in two ways: information can be conditioned, or it can be learned. The 'battle' between what dogs instinctively want to do and what we teach or train them to do takes place in a network of cells in the brain known as the limbic system. Dog owners and trainers override the limbic system by giving rewards to dogs for obeying their owners' commands rather than its own instincts.

Dogs have the same senses as man – sight, taste, scent, touch, and hearing – but every dog owner will also confirm that from their experience, dogs also have some 'special' senses which are also highly developed. Most often observed is a dog's ability to tell time! They always seem to know when it's time, say, for a child to come home from school and will often position themselves at a window to wait. Some researchers believe that the dog has an internal clock which functions to key the rhythms of its life to those of the household in which it lives, while others believe that they are close observers of routines and are reacting to clues which their owners may be unconsciously performing.

It is also widely believed that dogs are somewhat deficient in perceiving and recognizing forms. However, most owners will counter this argument with examples of their dogs reacting in excited expectation when a certain jacket, coat or pair of shoes are put on, which are worn for 'walkies' and not for going to work (which are ignored by the dog!) It could be argued that dogs are not responding to the forms themselves however, but to a range of perceptions including movements, smells, noises, and times of day which cue the excited anticipation of 'walkies'.

Eyes and Sight

While dogs' eyes are flatter than those of humans, and are able to change the shape of the lenses, thereby adjusting focal lengths, they are not quite as effective. On the other hand, dogs' eyes are much more receptive to light and movement than human eyes, but their resolving power is less efficient. This means that, while we humans can easily find a ball in long grass, a dog will have to 'snuffle' around to find it. Meanwhile, dogs are much more adept at spotting even the slightest movement from the corners of its eyes. A dog's facial anatomy is similar to that of its relative, the wolf, with widely spaced eyes for better lateral vision. This makes them more able to discern movements in the landscape. In

breeds where the eyes are more frontally placed, such as coursing dogs like greyhounds, these breeds are better able to focus on images and objects directly in front of them.

PERCEPTION IMPROVES IN DOGS WHEN BOTH THEY, AND THE OBJECT THEY ARE OBSERVING, ARE MOVING.

However, from experiments in perception, it seems that most dogs are completely confused when neither themselves nor objects are moving! Perception improves when the object moves, and is even better when the dog moves as well. This is because it is the basic instinct – shared also by humans – to 'freeze' in order to avoid detection.

Like other mammals, the retinas in dogs' eyes contain rods and cones: the rods are involved in night vision and, compared to humans, dogs have a far greater number of rods. The rods are also of use in daytime vision, because they are located on the outer edge of the retina and help in peripheral vision. The cones are concerned with daylight vision, but dogs do not have as many of these as humans so are less able to see such a full range of colors. Dogs, like cats, also have a third eyelid, called the nictitating membrane. This is 'hidden' under the lower eyelid and functions to sweep the eye clean while the lacrimal gland produces tears to lubricate the cornea.

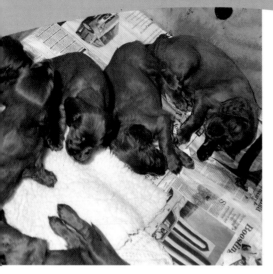

PUPPIES ARE BORN BOTH BLIND AND DEAF.

SHETLAND SHEEPDOG: SEMI-ERECT EARS THAT FOLD OVER AT THE TOP.

24

FRENCH BULLDOG WITH ITS DISTINCTIVE 'BAT' EARS.

Touch and Taste

Because puppies are both blind and deaf at birth, touch is the first sense to be developed and it remains a powerful and important sense throughout a dog's life. Above the eyes, around the muzzle and below the jaws are touch-sensitive hairs called vibrissae which sense changes in air flow, while each of the feet also have touch receptor nerves. Dogs have fewer taste buds than humans – for every six taste buds on the human tongue, dogs have only one. Nevertheless, while dogs are still able to distinguish sweet, salty, bitter, and sour tastes, it is more usual to regard a dog's responses to taste as either good, bad or indifferent!

Ear Shape and Hearing

Selective breeding has altered dogs' ears more than any other part of the body. The natural dog ear shape is that of the wolf, firmly erect and mobile. Many breeds today still maintain this ear shape in varying degrees: there are the pricked or erect German Shepherd-type ears, while the Doberman, which has naturally pendant ears that hang close to head, are in some countries, surgically amputated or 'lopped' to give a greater appearance of 'alertness'.

Other breeds have rose ears: these can be raised or laid back against the head and are to be found in breeds of racing dogs, or rose ears, which hang like petals at the side of the head. Ground-scenting dogs often have long, pendulous ears – sometimes touching the ground as it trails a scent. There are also semi-erect ears, which roll over at the tips – as on Shetland sheepdogs; erect and rounded 'bat' ears, such as in the French bulldog, and 'button' ears, that are erect but hang in a 'V' shape, such as in the Jack Russell terrier.

THE DOBERMAN HAS NATURALLY PENDANT EARS, WHICH ARE OFTEN SURGICALLY REMOVED TO MAKE THEM APPEAR MORE 'ALERT'.

THE JACK RUSSELL HAS 'BUTTON' EARS.

THE GERMAN SHEPHERD HAS NATURALLY ERECT EARS.

25

AS SOON AS PUPPIES LEARN TO HEAR AND SEE, THEY MUST LEARN TO RECOGNIZE THEIR MOTHER'S GROWLS AND BARKS.

Despite the variety of ear shapes, the anatomy of a dog's ear is very similar to that of a human's. Dogs do have much more mobile ears: dogs with erect ears can move them forwards or to the sides, and dogs with drooping, pendulous ears succeed to different degrees in erecting their ears to hear better. There are major differences in hearing ability: according to researchers, dogs are able to locate the source of a sound within six-hundredths of a second, and can hear sounds that are four times further away than humans can. Both low and high sounds require greater volume if they are to be heard and, in this respect, dogs and man are pretty much them same in terms of hearing. But dogs are able to hear very high-pitched sounds which are far above the range of man, and

which have brought about the so-called silent, or, Galton whistle: while the dog hears the whistle, the owner hears only the rush of air! At birth, puppies are deaf and blind, and their ears begin to open after about ten to twelve days, and then they must learn the meanings of their mother's growls and barks. This can be a painful experience, for often the mother will nip and bite her puppies as she growls to instruct them.

Scent

By far a dog's most advanced sense is that of scent, and a large proportion of the canine brain is devoted to processing information gained from sniffing and snuffling. The average dog has over 200 million scent receptors in its nasal folds compared to a human's mere five million. Moisture on dogs' noses helps capture scents, which are then sent to the nasal membranes which cover a series of very thin bones called turbinate bones. These bones are arranged so they have a number of 'folds', increasing the surface area so that even the minutest amount of scent is captured. In addition to the nose, dogs also have a sex-scent-capturing organ in the roof of their mouths which sends scent

information directly to the limbic system – the part of the dogs brain concerned with 'emotional' behavior.

By far the most interesting smells for dogs are urine, sweat, blood, decaying meat, and estral and anal gland secretions. The urine of female dogs contains a repellent secreted by the luteal glands in the ovaries, which keeps male dogs at bay. As a bitch (female) comes into estrous, or 'season', the luteal glands stop producing the repellent and it is replaced by other odors which are more 'attractive' to male dogs. The anal sacs are part of a dog's skin and sebaceous and sweat glands empty into each sac, which are located at the base of the anus. The secretions play a vital role in marking territory and in social recognition: when a dog passes a stool, muscles around the anal sacs squeeze out a few drops of the sticky secretion, making a 'marker' for other dogs to scent.

Dogs' noses are also able to discover information that is both local and transitory: wandering dogs urinate on lamp posts, car wheels, gates and fences, and mounds of earth. Another dog arriving on the scene will be able, through its sense of smell, to identify whether the first dog was male or female, the state of its health,

DOG SNIFFING: AN IMPORTANT METHOD OF FINDING INFORMATION.

hungry or well fed, or in estrous. By the tracks made by the first dog, which have left sweat deposits and perhaps soil from other places, it will know whether the first dog was local or a newcomer – and it will be able to follow the scent to find out exactly where this new dog has gone!

DOGS SNIFF EACH OTHER WHEN THEY MEET FOR THE FIRST TIME.

27

SHORT AND CURLY

Skin and Coat

Like humans, a dog's skin is made up of two structures, the surface, or epidermis, and the underlying flexible and elastic dermis. The dermis provides blood and nerve supplies to the epidermis and, in the dermis, there are numerous skin glands, the most common of which are the sebaceous glands which secrete into the hair follicles, nourishing and lubricating the hairs. Inside the ear canal, the sebaceous glands have been modified to produce cerumin, or wax, while other hair follicles, such as those in the footpads, have sweat glands.

The coats of hair that dogs have vary more than any other species of domestic animal. This is because many hairs of different texture can, in fact, grow from an individual follicle. The central hair growing from a follicle is surrounded by up to five primary hairs, each with its own sebaceous gland, sweat gland and *arrector pili*, or erector muscle. The erector muscle enables dogs to lift or raise the hairs on their bodies to varying degrees. While we often say that our hair 'stood on end', for the most part, unlike dogs, we are getting goose-flesh or goose-pimples! In some instances these primary hairs can be surrounded by further, small, secondary hairs, each with a lubricating sebaceous gland – but no sweat glands or erector muscles – so these secondary hairs cannot be raised. There are also 'hairless' dogs which have appeared in many parts of the world, such as the Chinese crested, and Mexican hairless dog. The cause of this hairlessness is not entirely known: it has been

LONG AND LUXURIOUS.

attributed to a number of causes including blood factor deficiencies, skin ailments involving pigmentation, and to genetic accidents caused by human intervention. All the hairless breeds, however, give birth to some pups with hair, which are called 'powder puffs'.

SPITZ-TYPE DOGS EVOLVED IN THE ARCTIC CIRCLE AND SO HAVE DENSE COATS FOR INSULATION.

CHINESE CRESTED: A HAIRLESS BREED.

Textures

The primary hairs in a dog's coat are often called guard hairs or topcoat, and the secondary hairs are often called down or undercoat. The density of these hairs and the way they are distributed, are influential factors with regard to

THE LONG COAT OF THE YORKSHIRE TERRIER IS A MODERN DEVELOPMENT FOR SHOWING THE BREED.

coat types. While a Yorkshire terrier has around 100 hairs per square centimetre (half an inch), a Sptiz-type dog will have around 600 hairs. Some breeds, like wire-haired dogs, have more primary hairs and fewer secondary hairs, providing for a tough, insulating coat that is also good protection from scratches and bites. Other breeds have more soft secondary hairs, and these dogs generally have evolved in warmer climates. Looked at under a microscope, the straight, coarse outer coat of many breeds are made of hairs which are round, while 'woolly' hairs are elliptical in section and wavy, or slightly curling hairs, are oval. In addition to the normal coat hairs, (which are grown and shed in cycles depending on reactions to temperature changes, growth in daylight hours, hormonal activity, as well as dietary and stress factors) there are single tyrotrich hairs scattered all over a dog's body.

These, along with the vibrissae hairs – the stiff 'whisker' type hairs, act as specialized touch receptors, controlled by the sympathetic nervous system.

As with cats, the coat colors of dogs are so varied that often one word is not enough to describe them. Dog breeders have developed a whole range of technical terms to describe colors and they range from the ordinary – grey, cream, and red- to the poetic – wheaten, lemon, ivory, and cinnamon. Then there's Blenheim (chestnut and white markings), blue-merle (marbled blue and grey mixed with black), dappled, flecked, tricolor (black, white, and tan), grizzled (a mixture of colors including bluish-grey, red, and black), pied (unequally proportioned patches of white and another color), roan (a fine mix of colored hairs alternating with white hairs) and sable (black-tipped hairs against a background of a gold, silver, grey, fawn, or tan basic coat).

THE VARIOUS COAT TEXTURES OF DIFFERENT BREEDS ARE RELATED TO THE DOGS' ORIGINS, AND HAVE BEEN INFLUENCED BY CLIMATE AND OCCUPATION.

Walkies!

A healthy dog has a perfectly co-ordinated movement and a smooth gait. Under the paws, nails, and pads of the feet are skin structures that have been modified. The nails are produced from a modified extension of the epidermis. The footpads are cushions on the underside of the toes and are covered with a thick and protective horny skin. The pads contain sweat-producing glands, which help keep them supple and leave scent traces on the ground. Unlike human hands and feet, a dog's footpads are much less sensitive to heat and cold. On the inner side of each forefoot, corresponding with the human thumb in position, is a dew claw. In most breeds the dew claws are removed a few days after birth in order to give a cleaner line to the leg. There are some breeds, however, where dew claws are essential to the breed standard: the alapaha blue blood bulldog never has its dew claws amputated, the Icelandic sheepdog and the Lundehund both have double dew claws on their front paws, while the Portuguese watchdog has dew claws present on the hind legs, as does the Beauceron.

A HEALTHY, ENERGETIC DOG.

In normal, healthy dogs, there are four varieties of movement: the leisurely gait (with frequent stops for investigating interesting or exciting new scents!); the fast walk, or trot; the lope, or canter; and, the gallop, or run.

GETTING UP SPEED.

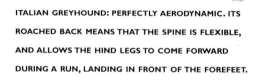

During the slow walk, three of the dog's four feet are normally in contact with the ground: this is known as three-point suspension. During the trot, or fast walk, only two feet are on the ground at the same time and the legs move in the following order: left hind and left front – LF and RH, RF and RH, RF and LH. The forefoot on one side is lifted before the hind foot reaches the ground so the dog's body rolls towards the side for a split moment as it is left unsupported. The front end of the dog's body, which is heavier than the back, drops forward slightly and the head automatically jerks. A perfectly balanced gait – such as that demonstrated by champions in the show ring – is when there is perfect synchronisation between the two halves of the body – regardless of whether the 'bisection' is transverse (across the dog's waist) or longitudinally (along the body length).

In trotting, or the fast walk, the dog's body weight falls on 'diagonal' limbs since the order of movement is: LF and RH together, followed by RF and LH together. For just a fraction of a second in the trot, all four feet are momentarily clear of the ground.

ITALIAN GREYHOUND: PERFECTLY AERODYNAMIC. ITS ROACHED BACK MEANS THAT THE SPINE IS FLEXIBLE, AND ALLOWS THE HIND LEGS TO COME FORWARD DURING A RUN, LANDING IN FRONT OF THE FOREFEET.

In the lope or canter, the order of movement begins first with all four feet on the ground, then: LH alone, LF and both H, LF and RH, both F, and RH and RF.

In breeds such as greyhounds, during the gallop, the hind feet pass forwards and land in front of the forefeet. Because these dogs have a flexible spine, when they run or jump, the hinder parts of their body operate as an extension of their hind legs – in other words their lower back operates as a second thigh muscle! The gallop is an almost continuous series of leaps through the air.

Chapter 2
Breeding

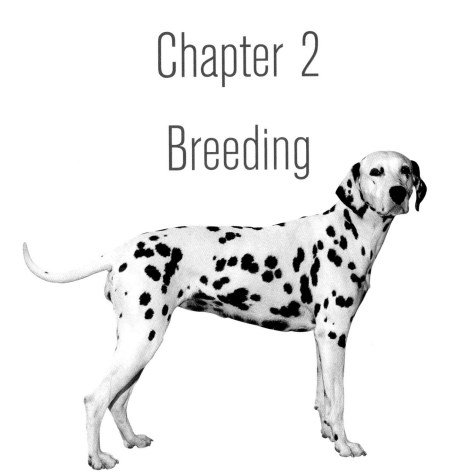

Selective Breeding

The huge variety of shapes, sizes, colors, coats, temperaments, and skills – such as enhanced scenting, herding, pointing, setting, retrieving and racing – are evidence of the 'flexible' nature of canine genes, and also of the skills of breeders over thousands of years. Today, most dogs are bred to Kennel Club (K.C.)standards rather than to working standards, and this means that many of today's dogs may look markedly different to even their recent ancestors. So-called 'breed histories' are often little more than entertaining legends because one difficulty in compiling any authentic histories of dog breeds is that, prior to 1873, there were no Kennel Clubs anywhere in the world. Consequently, before this time, there were very few systems of registration or accurate records of breeds.

Breeders select dogs for breeding mainly by their appearance and behavior, as well as on their relationship to outstanding individuals – both ancestral and contemporary. All controlled, or selective, breeding implies selection – and rejection. Some dogs and bitches are allowed to have offspring, others are not. Through selection, breeders 'push' the breed into the desired direction in order to maintain the standards and quality of the breeds. This

must be done carefully as, otherwise, valuable canine qualities may be lost and, worse, genetic faults may be perpetuated and increased. Many faults are recessive, that is, the animal that has the fault must be carrying a gene for the condition in its duplex form. This can be the result of inbreeding, where two close relatives have been mated, thereby increasing the chances of the offspring inheriting the same genetic pattern from both parents. In other words, it tends to increase what is called homozygosity. Some inbreeding – often extensive – has been used at some time or another to produce almost all the breeds of domestic livestock, including dogs. Most modern breeders, aware of the dangers of inbreeding, practice line breeding instead, which is the mating of individuals tracing back to one or more notably good common ancestors.

GRAND BASSET GRIFFON VANDÉEN

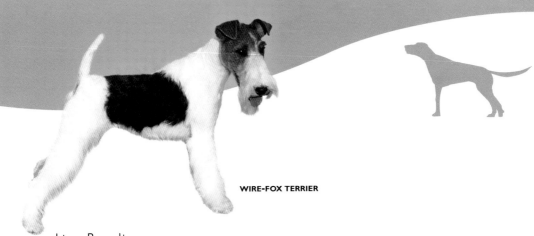

WIRE-FOX TERRIER

Line Breeding

This is the mating of two animals that are related – but not so closely that they are mother and son, or father and daughter.

If the parents are A and B, one or more outstanding dogs recur in the pedigree of a line-bred dog.

The dog on the diagram marked with dots occurs three times in the pedigree of

the offspring of parents A and B, and the whole genetic inheritance of the offspring comes from three dogs (colored black, white and dotted on the diagram) without crosses (the mating of unrelated individuals of the same breed, marked O) four generations back.

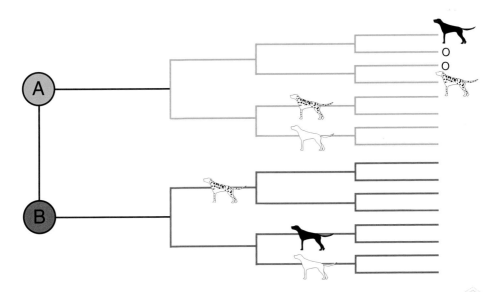

The Role of The Kennel Clubs

For thousands of years, emperors and kings, generals, war lords and rulers had hunting and fighting dogs. While they were prized for their skills, they were also bred for their looks. The elite in society set the trends in fashions for their nobles to follow and new 'trends' were started such as 'lap dogs' or companions for the ladies of the courts.

By the 19th century, ownership of dogs had spread to all classes in society, but the ownership of selectively bred dogs was most common among the more affluent. The first dog show in England was more of a social affair: held by English aristocrats, the aim was to raise money for charity. By 1860, however, the first true dog-show society was

born in Birmingham, England and three years later, in Paris, France, the Acclimation Societé, held the first dog show in continental Europe.

The exact definition of a 'breed' was still open to definition: there were hundreds of variations in sizes, shapes, and colors of dogs within a single breed. The many conflicting opinions on how a particular type of dog should look eventually led to the establishment of canine societies and 'kennel clubs', which started to 'fix' official standards or 'ideals' by which a dog could be classified and judged. In 1873 a Kennel Club was formed in England. As well as producing a stud book containing the pedigrees of over 4,000 dogs divided into 40 breeds, the Kennel Club also produced a framework of rules and regulations within

The main aims of the British Kennel Club are to:

- Classify breeds
- Register pedigree dogs
- Oversee the transfer of ownership of registered dogs
- Register and license breed clubs, canine societies and dog-training societies
- License and control dog shows, field, working and obedience trials
- Promote in every way the general improvement of dogs
- Devise and enforce Kennel Club rules
- Present awards

which dog shows and trials could be held. In 1880, the Kennel Club decided that no dog could be exhibited at a show held under its rules unless the dog had been registered with the Kennel Club. This ruling was to have the greatest effect on the future of selective breeding of dogs worldwide because it now defined a breed as a group of dogs recognized by them.

The Kennel Club set the pattern for later clubs: in 1882 the Societé Centrale Canine was founded in France and, a year later, the American Kennel Club (A.K.C.) was founded. Both these clubs, along with the later Féderation Cynologique Internationale (F.C.I.) formed in 1911 (under the watchful eye of German, French, Austrian, Dutch, and Belgian kennel clubs) required that only dogs registered with their respective clubs could be shown at their shows. The F.C.I. member countries now include most European and Scandinavian countries as well as reciprocal agreements with southeast Asian nations, Japan, Central and Southern American countries, and with the United Kingdom. The F.C.I. works to the mutual acknowledgment of stud books, to agree on breed standards and to adopt international rules and judges.

Cruft's: the Greatest (Dog) Show on Earth

Born in 1851, Charles Cruft worked as a shop assistant with James Spratt, who had brought back from America a newfangled idea: the dog biscuit. As Cruft progressed in the trade, he began to travel and visited the Paris Exhibition in 1879, where he was asked to organize a dog show. Back in London, in 1886, Cruft went on to organize the Allied Terrier Show, which was a great success and convinced Cruft to make a long-term contract at the Agricultural Hall in Islington, north London. In 1891, the first of the world-famous Cruft's Dog Shows was held. Queen Victoria was a patron and a visitor to the shows and, until the United Kingdom introduced strict quarantine laws, Cruft's shows attracted entries from across Europe, Russia and even as far afield as India. Following Cruft's death in 1938, the Kennel Club acquired the show which is visited by an estimated 50,000 visitors. Such is the interest in the show, and in the popularity of the dog ultimately selected to be the Supreme Champion, that the event always makes the national television news headlines.

Classification of Breeds

HOUND

The classification of breeds and breed types is quite arbitrary. The ancient Romans classified dogs as 'house dogs,' 'shepherd dogs,' and 'sporting dogs,' and even in the late Middle Ages when Dr. Caius made his classification, he divided them into three groups: 'hunters,' 'homely dogs,' and 'curs'. The three groups were further subdivided: hunters were divided into terriers, harriers, bloodhounds, gazehounds, greyhounds, spaniels, setters, and water spaniels. Homely dogs also found 'gentle' spaniels included, as well as dogs described as 'comforters', while curs were divided into shepherds, mastiffs and 'bandogges' – an ancient term for a dog that was tied up by day and released at night, the medieval equivalent of a modern, trained professional guard dog.

In the 1700s the Swedish scientist Dr. Carolus Linneaus (1702–1778) published his text The System of Nature in which he listed and named 35 breeds of dog, while the French naturalist, the Comte de Buffon (1707–1788) further classified dogs into five groups according to their shape and behavior. In the following century, as the interest in science grew, new breed classifications were explored and, in 1878, the German scientist Professor Fitzinger classified 180 dog breeds and varieties according to their external features.

Even with the founding of the world's first Kennel Club in 1873, all dogs were shown together. Soon, however, two categories of dogs were devised, called simply 'sporting' and 'non-sporting'. Sporting dogs were soon subdivided and had three groups: gundogs, hounds, and terriers. Non-sporting dogs proved a little more difficult to classify, but eventually, toy dogs were separated out, followed by working dogs and the miscellaneous breeds, labelled as utility dogs. In the U.S.,

GUN DOG

TOY (KING CHARLES)

gundogs are still known as 'sporting dogs' and utility dogs as 'non-sporting dogs).

Today the K.C. has breed standards for six main groups of dogs: hounds, terriers, gundogs, utility, toy, and working dogs. Each of the original breed clubs retains the rights to define the standards for their own breed of dog, but all the clubs that are affiliated to the F.C.I. submit their standards to them for international recognition. This does mean that the F.C.I. may recognize certain breeds of dogs, while the K.C. in the UK and the A.K.C. (American Kennel Club) may not! Furthermore, the breed standards are often interpreted in different ways in different countries, so there may be distinctive differences in appearances between dogs from different countries.

The F.C.I. classification of breeds is a complicated one, based on the origins and physical characteristics of the breeds as well as on their behavior. In its most basic form, the F.C.I. classification contains eight categories, which, once again, are arbitrary since some breeds could very accurately be included in another category! The eight F.C.I. categories are:

BASENJI

Primitive dogs (once again an arbitrary classification applied to a small group of dogs descended from *Canus lupus pallipes*, or the Indian Plains wolf. The group includes 'genuine primitives' such as the dingo and the New Guinea singing dog, as well as the basenji and Mexican hairless dogs, both of which are the result of human intervention in breeding); sight hounds; scent hounds; spitz-type dogs; terriers; gundogs; livestock dogs; and, companion dogs.

Chapter 3
Dog Breeds

Gun Dogs

CURLY—COATED RETRIEVER

Throughout the great part of man's history of hunting for food – and for sport – it was sight and scent hounds that accompanied them. Such hounds were the preserve of the nobility and rich land-owning classes, and were used for hunting 'large game' such as deer or wild boar, while the lower orders in society were largely prohibited from owning and using them. The peasant and farming classes developed their own 'hunting dogs' – terriers that would hunt 'vermin' by digging and tunnelling after smaller mammals such as rats, rabbits, or foxes.

The introduction of firearms encouraged breeders to take a further, deeper interest in the natural instincts of hounds and terriers to scent, track, 'go to earth' and even to swim. What was needed now were dogs that could find game, but would then stand or crouch stock still, or, on command, leap into icy water to 'retrieve' shot game – not eat the game, but deliver the dead animal back to the hunter. This type of dog not only had the natural instincts that hounds and terriers already demonstrated, but also needed a willingness to be trained. In the

16th and 17th centuries, using a genetic base derived from hounds and dogs with a 'herding instinct', breeders developed some 50 breeds of gun dogs. These gun dogs are usually divided into five subgroups: water dogs, pointers, setters, flushing dogs and retrievers.

Water dogs, which will retrieve shot game from rivers and lakes, require both an urge to swim and a tight, waterproof coat, like that of the curly-coated retriever. Pointers and setters were employed originally to accompany hunters armed with nets. The dogs followed the air scent of game, silently searched for the animal on the ground and then stopped in their tracks and remained completely still: the pointer freezes with one of its forelegs 'bent' and 'points' at the quarry; the setter works in the same manner except that it crouches down or 'sets'. In both cases, the dog's natural instinct to capture the prey has been 'stopped' by training.

Flushing dogs work their way through dense

CLUMBER SPANIEL

FIELD SPANIEL

undergrowth and 'flush' the game birds towards the hunters. At one time all British spaniels were classified as land, field, or water spaniels depending on the terrain in which they worked, but with developments in breeding for show standards, classifications became more 'distinct': English and Welsh 'springers' (so called because their flushing technique also involved 'springing' birds into nets) were separated from the 'cockers' (so called because their small size made them suitable for small game such as woodcock), while field, Sussex and clumber spaniels became distinct breeds.

LABRADOR RETRIEVER

Using the water–loving dogs of Newfoundland (see page 74), British breeders developed retrievers. These dogs had the natural ability to carry game 'softly' in their mouths — without marking them with their teeth — coupled with the dog's great intelligence, and a willingness to learn and obey. These outstanding qualities, seen in Labrador retrievers and golden retrievers not only makes them popular gun dogs, but firm favorites as family pets, and as 'service dogs' — in particular, as guide dogs for the blind.

SPRINGER SPANIEL

English Cocker Spaniel

Other Names: **Cocker spaniel**
Date of Origin: **19th century**
Place of Origin: **Great Britain**
Original Use: **Small game flushing and retrieving**
Modern Use: **Companion**
Size: Height: **15–16 in.**
      Weight: **28–32 lb**
Colors: **Various including black, red, blue roan,
      strawberry roan, black-and-white, and tricolor**
Recognized by: **A.K.C., K.C.**

The term 'spaniel' has been in use since the Renaissance and it refers to the original home of the breed, Spain, which in the 16th century was at the height of its cultural and political powers and where the 'new' methods of hunting and the dog breeds were first developed. Such dogs were well established on the Continent and were probably known in England during the reign of the Plantagenet kings (from 1154–1485). The term 'spaniel' was however generic: in the 17th century both 'large' and 'small' spaniels were evident, as well as those with either long or short bodies which were 'fast' or 'slow' dogs. From the melting pot of spaniels the distinct breeds such as the English and American cocker spaniels, the Sussex, the springer, and the field spaniels were developed.

The cocker is said by some to have earned its name because it was used for small game bird hunting, such as woodcock, while others maintain it was because the spaniel 'sprung', 'started' or 'cocked' the game – first for the net, and later for the gun. Whatever the origins, the name was so widely used that, in 1873, the English Kennel Club recognized the breed under that name.

Game hunters claim that the cocker is the most efficiently designed of all the spaniels: robust and strong, but small enough to push through dense undergrowth, a neck that is strong enough to lift game that is large and heavy relative to the dog itself, and long enough to keep the game lifted clear of the floor in the retrieve. The forelegs are solid and short – perfect for concentrated power – while the elegantly shaped head has a well-defined, square muzzle and a well-developed nose.

American Cocker Spaniel

Other Names: **Cocker spaniel**
Date of Origin: **19th century**
Place of Origin: **United States of America**
Original Use: **Small game retrieving**
Modern Use: **Companion**
Size: Height: **14–15 in.**
      Weight: **24–28 lb**
Colors: **Variety**
Recognized by: **A.K.C., K.C.**

'Cocker spaniel' is in fact the proper name for two distinct breeds: the English cocker spaniel and the American cocker. The English cocker is the older of the two breeds, although legend tells of how the American cocker's ancestor arrived in the New World with the Pilgrim Fathers aboard the Mayflower in 1620. While the term spaniel had been in use in England in the Middle Ages, the real history of the cocker spaniel begins with the birth of a dog called 'Obo' in 1879 and all cockers, English or American, can trace their ancestry back to him.

The American cocker spaniel was developed in the U.S.A. from the working English cocker, but while the American cocker still retains its hunting instincts and attempts have been made to work dogs, its greatest appeal lies in the gentle, loyal and affectionate companionship the American cocker offers as a household pet. In the 1920s American breeders developed cockers with a more distinctly domed head to the English cocker, and one which displayed more height at the shoulder, a shorter back and a slightly longer neck. The American cocker is also distinguished by its' beautiful long, silky, and wavy coat of dense, fine hair which needs careful grooming on a daily basis to prevent it from matting.

Regrettably, the American cocker spaniel, like its English cousin, does suffer from a range of health problems including skin and eye complaints and, sometimes, epilepsy. Despite these problems, the American cocker spaniel, with its wonderful character, remains one of America's most popular 'home-grown' breeds.

Clumber Spaniel

Other Names: **None**
Date of Origin: **19th century**
Place of Origin: **Nottinghamshire, England**
Original Use: **Tracking, game retrieving**
Modern Use: **Tracking, companion**
Size: Height: **19–20 in.**
      Weight: **65–80 lb**
Colors: **Plain white (lemon markings permitted)**
Recognized by: **A.K.C., K.C.**

The clumber is the heavyweight of the spaniel world. They are both large and deceptively slow moving – except when you want to catch up with one! The clumber is named after the Duke of Newcastle's Nottinghamshire estate, Clumber Park. According to legend, this spaniel's ancestors were retrievers owned by the French Duc de Noialles, who, at the outbreak of the French Revolution, sent his dogs to safety in England. The clumber's ancestors may, therefore, include the basset hound – which would account for its long back – and the St. Bernard, which would account for the very large, square–shaped head.

A more likely explanation however, is that the clumber was bred in Nottinghamshire using existing dogs in the region, which would rule out the St. Bernard as a possible influence. Whatever dogs were used, the aim was to produce a gun dog that would be less volatile during a shoot than other breeds, and whose speed was dictated by its size: in essence the clumber was 'designed' to flatten the dense undergrowth to a suitable width, allowing the armed huntsmen on foot (and who, in the 19th century, were also large in the girth) to follow at a decent 'leisurely' pace! Working clumber spaniels operate as a team, rather leisurely beating the game towards the hunters.

This gentlemanly pace of the shoot ensured that the clumber became a firm favorite with the royals: King Edward VII, a dedicated huntsman and *bon viveur*, who earned himself the nickname of 'Tum–Tum' on account of his ever increasing waist,

was particularly fond of the clumber spaniel and he kept a large number of them at Sandringham, in Norfolk. Later, King George V also used clumbers exclusively on the royal estates in Norfolk, and the bloodline of these dogs was a great influence on the breed. Today, the preference for working spaniels is for faster animals which can cover more ground, and the clumber spaniel is more likely to be found tracking and retrieving sticks and fallen leaves in back yards!

Field Spaniel

Other Names: **None**
Date of Origin: **19th century**
Place of Origin: **Great Britain**
Original Use: **Game retrieving**
Modern Use: **Companion**
Size: Height: **20–23 in.**
    Weight: **35–50 lb**
Colors: **Black, roan, liver**
Recognized by: **A.K.C., K.C.**

The field spaniel, although popular in the early part of the 20th century, is now quite a rare dog. The breed has an ancestry similar to that of the cocker spaniel and both, in their early days, were classed simply as either 'field spaniels under 25 lb' and 'field spaniels over 25 lb'. In 1892, however, the two breeds were separated as distinct as cocker spaniel and field spaniel. While the cocker became shorter and a more robust dog, breeders of field spaniels worked towards producing low, long dogs with heavy-boned legs. These dogs looked more like heavily built dachshunds than working dogs and, consequently, the field spaniel lost the greater part of its ability to work outside of the show ring.

By the end of World War II, the field spaniel was nearly extinct, but was saved by the efforts of breeders who rescued the breed from complete obscurity. In the 1960s numbers were increased after breeders introduced English cocker spaniels (see page 44) and springer spaniels (see page 52) in order to regenerate the breed and produce today's good looking and affectionate dog.

Field spaniels today have a moderate length body that is well ribbed and carried on strong, muscular hind quarters and straight front legs. The shoulders slope well back while the skull is well developed with a distinct occiput. Like all spaniels, the field's ears are long, wide and beautifully feathered. The glorious silky and glossy coat is flat, but can be slightly waved, and dense enough to resist wet weather. Field spaniels should always be 'self colored' (solid, or 'whole' colored): black, liver, roan or any of these colors with tan markings over their rather serious–looking eyes, on the cheeks, feet and pasterns.

Sussex Spaniel

Other Names: **None**
Date of Origin: **18th century**
Place of Origin: **Hastings, Sussex, England**
Original Use: **Game tracking**
Modern Use: **Companion**
Size: Height: **15–16 in.**
       Weight: **40–50 lb**
Colors: **Golden–liver**
Recognized by: **A.K.C., K.C.**

In 1795, Mr. Fuller of Rosehill Park, Hastings in East Sussex, England began breeding dogs for a special purpose: gun dogs to work in districts where the terrain was rough and the undergrowth very dense. What was most needed in the dog was strength and the ability to 'give tongue'– a trait not desirable in other spaniels but one which in the county of Sussex at least, was highly desirable. This is because in such dense undergrowth of bracken and brambles where dogs couldn't be seen, they at least could be heard and the experienced hunter was able to distinguish the quarry of the dog – whether it is 'furred' or 'feathered' – from the variations in the tone of the Sussex's voice. Mr. Fuller's breed was the result of crossing various existing spaniels, including the now extinct liver-and-white Norfolk, the field spaniel (see page 48) and possibly, some early 'springing' spaniels. The result was a dog of the most gorgeous color – and a color unknown inn any other breed – a rich 'golden-liver' which shades to gold at the tips of the hairs. The Sussex first reached the show rings in 1862 in London but occupied such a modest place in the dog world that World War I threatened their existence. A brief recovery in the 1920s and 1930s was set back once again by the outbreak of World War II: in 1947 only 10 Sussex spaniels were registered in the English Kennel Club. Accidental inbreeding and selective breeding among such few specimens is a hazardous affair and, consequently, inherited defects such as drooping lower eyelids and flews are common, and such conditions can lead to infections.

Today, this rare breed is safeguarded by only handful of dedicated breeders, largely in the U.S.A., so the Sussex continues to be rare – and even rarer in its homeland of England.

English Springer Spaniel

Other Names: **Spaniel**
Date of Origin: **17th century**
Place of Origin: **Great Britain**
Original Use: **Game flushing, retrieving**
Modern Use: **Gundog, companion**
Size: Height: **19–20 in.**
Weight: **49–53 lb**
Colors: **Black-white, liver-white**
Recognized by: **A.K.C., K.C.**

Many claim that the English springer spaniel is the oldest of all the sporting spaniels. Long before the invention of firearms, spaniels were used to spring or flush game, causing it to leave cover so that a hunter's waiting hawks and falcons could swoop in on the quarry. Spaniels were also used to 'spring' birds and small mammals into nets, hence 'springer spaniels'. There is uncertainty as to what these early dogs actually looked like: it was not until the 19th century, and the formation of dog shows, that the spaniels began to be separated into 'land' and 'water' spaniels. Land spaniels were divided into categories according to their weight, and the English springer spaniel emerged in the heaviest classes, as distinct from the cockers.

Today, the English springer spaniel is still

Britain's most popular working spaniel: an all-rounder in the field with seemingly unlimited stamina and a great love of the water. It is the tallest in the leg – and the raciest – of all the British land spaniels and one of the most intelligent. Consequently, these dogs need constant mental and physical activity to keep them from being bored. The show and working strains in the breed have become quite distinct: the show dogs are bigger in general and have heavier bones: they are especially good at retrieving tennis balls in parks, and find it difficult to resist duck ponds!

The most commonly seen coat color in English springer spaniels is liver and white, but black and white is also acceptable, as are these colors combined with tan markings. Their straight coats are firm and require regular grooming.

Welsh Springer Spaniel

The Principality of Wales has given the canine world three breeds: the Welsh terrier, the Welsh corgis (see page 245) and the Welsh springer spaniel. Three dogs – though not these three breeds – were mentioned in the Laws of Howel Dda, a 10th century ruler of Wales. The three dogs mentioned were a 'tracker', a 'greyhound' and a 'spaniel'. This last dog is described further as being of equal value to a stallion or the king's 'buck hound' (a buck is a male deer).

The mention of a spaniel is curious at this time because it predates the introduction of Spanish dogs to Britain.

Other Names: Once known as the Welsh cocker
Date of Origin: 17th century
Place of Origin: Wales, Great Britain
Original Use: Game flushing, retrieving
Modern Use: Gun dog, companion
Size: Height: 18–19 in.
       Weight: 135–45 lb
Colors: Red-white
Recognized by: A.K.C., K.C.

Even more curious, an old Welsh law dating from AD 300 also mentions 'our native spaniel'. Most people in Britain would not have known of the existence of Spain at this time so it seems that both the breed and the name here are unconnected with Iberia. One theory is that these spaniels came to Wales from Gaul ('ancient' France) in pre-Roman times and consequently the Welsh springer spaniel may well share a common ancestry with the equally ancient and similarly colored, Brittany (see page 55).

While never a 'popular' dog, the Welsh springer spaniel has always been a highly respected working dog, capable of

driving herds of cattle or sheep and excelling at flushing or 'springing' game birds. The coloring of the Welsh springer spaniel is very distinctive: it was commented upon by Dr. Caius, in his book *English Dogges* of c.1570, who wrote of Spaniels whose 'skins are white and if they are marked with any spottes, they are commonly red'. Dr. Caius did however mention how remarkably white — almost pearly white — the white part of the coat was. Such a distinctive appearance made the dog attractive also to artists: they make numerous appearances in the sporting prints of the 18th century and in a number of family portraits by such artists as John Copley and Joseph Wright.

The flat, silky coat is less profuse on the Welsh's legs and ears than on some other breeds, and it stays quite clean because of its natural oiliness — for this dog is also a fine retriever from water. The ears are also an unusual shape: smaller than an English springer's, they are best described as shaped like a 'vine leaf'. When they were first introduced into the show ring, they were known as 'Welsh cockers'. In 1902, the Kennel Club recognized their existence as 'Welsh springers' and as a breed distinct from the cocker spaniel (see page 44).

Brittany Spaniel

Other Names: **Armoricon, Armorique, Epagneul Breton, Brittany**
Date of Origin: **18th century**
Place of Origin: **Brittany, France**
Original Use: **Retrieving**
Modern Use: **Retrieving, companion**
Size: Height: **18–20½ in.**
   Weight: **28–33 lb**
Colors: **Black-white, liver-white, tricolor**
Recognized by: **A.K.C., K.C.**

Originating in the region in northern France from which it takes its name, the Brittany is the breed which 'bridges the gap' between the spaniels and the setters and pointers. Spaniels work within the range of the gun and flush birds inside that range, which works well when there is dense ground cover hiding lots of birds. On more open ground, such as moorlands, a faster and lighter dog is needed – one that is capable of covering a greater range. Pointers and setters are such dogs: quartering the ground in front of the guns, scenting the air with wide nostrils to find hidden birds. In this way, the dogs will find sitting birds often at some distance from the guns: when they do, they point or set the bird, standing or crouching in a rigid position that indicates the bird's location and with luck, keeps the bird there until the guns come into range. The most popular native breed in France, and still a working dog there, as well as in Canada and the United States, the Brittany is the only spaniel breed that points – and probably the world's only 'stumpy–tailed' pointer as well! The dog is born either tailless or, if it is naturally long, the tail is docked to 4 in; the ears are also shorter than those of other spaniels and are set above eye level.

Like the English, the French developed sporting dogs to suit the regions in which they worked, but in the 19th century, British breeders crossed the Channel to France to shoot woodcocks and took with them their own dogs, especially setters. It seems that, from crossings between the English dogs and the local Breton spaniels, the breed known as the Armorique emerged, until in 1905, it was officially recognized as the Brittany Spaniel.

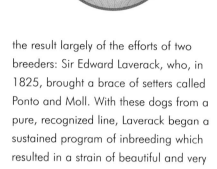

English Setter

Other Names: Setting spaniel
Date of Origin: 19th century
Place of Origin: Great Britain
Original Use: Game retrieving, bird setting
Modern Use: Retrieving, companion
Size: Height: 24–27 in.
         Weight: 55–66 lb
Colors: Tricolor, lemon-white, black-white, liver-white
Recognized by: A.K.C., K.C.

The English setter, with its delicate dappling or 'freckles' and shading of colors, has a very long history: a bond signed in 1485 by a Mr. John Harris states that, in exchange for 10 shillings (about a dollar) he could keep 'certain spaniels to set partridges, pheasants and other game' for six months. These dogs, called 'setting spaniels', had their names later shortened to 'setter', and finally to English setter, to distinguish them from the many other types that evolved during the same period. Such setting spaniels were longer in the leg than today's spaniel breeds, but they did work with the same lashing tails that setters do when quartering the ground. Until the 19th century, however, these setters were not the beautiful, elegant or swift-footed dogs we know today. The modern English setter is

the result largely of the efforts of two breeders: Sir Edward Laverack, who, in 1825, brought a brace of setters called Ponto and Moll. With these dogs from a pure, recognized line, Laverack began a sustained program of inbreeding which resulted in a strain of beautiful and very able dogs.

Inbreeding fixes the virtues or 'positive points' in a breed; but, while inbreeding does not introduce faults in dogs, it can, and does, intensify existing faults.

Consequently, while the breeding program succeeded in producing an elegant, easily trainable dog that was an excellent worker in the field, it also meant that the English setter can suffer inherited diseases: allergic skin reactions are common in predominantly white-colored dogs and, in all varieties, there is a tendency to blindness caused by the deterioration of the retinas. The development of the English setter was continued shortly afterwards by Sir Purcell Llewellin who successfully continued the long-term breeding program.

The modern English setter is shorter in the leg than its ancestors – and the other setter breeds – since it was developed to work on grassland and stubble rather than rough moorlands and bog, where they pointed out game in the traditional manner, and then, on command, stealthily inched forward towards the game until the bird broke cover.

In the 20th century, the use of the English setter as a gun dog in Britain declined and, today, it is no longer used. In the United States and Canada however, the breed split into two different types: smaller strains were developed for hunting and field trials, making the English setter one of the most popular breeds of hunting dogs among the bird dogs, while the larger dog is reserved for show.

Gordon Setter

Other Names: **Black-and-tan setter**
Date of Origin: **18th century**
Place of Origin: **Banffshire, Scotland**
Original Use: **Bird setting**
Modern Use: **Gun dog, companion**
Size: Height: **24–26 in.**
    Weight: **56–65 lb**
Colors: **Black with tan markings**
Recognized by: **A.K.C., K..C.**

The Gordon setter is the largest, strongest, heaviest and slowest of the setters. It is also the only gun dog to be produced by Scotland – in spite of the country's strong sporting traditions. In fact, the Gordon setter is a very versatile gun dog: they are hardy enough to endure the harsh Scottish weather of early season shoots; they can withstand the heat of an summer shoot (the season starts on the 'Glorious 12th August); they can go without water for long periods and their legs and feet are strong enough to work over baked fields and the most brittle and prickly stubble. Scotland really had no need of other gun dogs when it had the magnificent Gordon setter already!

Black-and-tan setters existed in Britain in the 17th century, but the Gordon setter was developed and established by Alexander, 4th Duke of Richmond and Gordon, at his estate in Banffshire in Scotland, who continued to perfect the breed until his death in 1827. It is believed that the Gordon setter is the result of a cross between the Black-and-tan setter and bloodhounds (see page 107). This would account for the color – and the Gordon's habit of hunting with its nose to the ground. There is also reputed to be collie (see page 230) blood: local history relates that one of the Duke's shepherds owned a black 'colley' who was a natural at finding game – even when the Duke's setters had failed! Moreover, this 'colley' froze and pointed, which earned her invitations to the ducal shoots and, it seems, to the kennels. This would also seem to account for the Gordon's earlier tendency: on finding game, the Gordon tended to circle it – like a sheepdog – holding the game in place

rather than the more usual 'setting'. Moving around the game would be dangerous for the dog as it could end up on the 'wrong' side, in the line of fire. Through breeding, and with careful training, this tendency has now been eliminated.

The magnificent coat, jet black in color with rich chestnut-tan markings, is fairly flat and a moderate length on the body. Elsewhere – on the head, front of the legs and tips of the ears – it is short and fine. The feathering on the belly, chest and throat makes a wonderful 'fringe'. The tail is fairly short and straight and is carried horizontal or just below the line of the back.

Irish Setter

Other Names: Modder rhu (Gaelic for 'red dog'), red setter

Date of Origin: 18th century

Place of Origin: Ireland

Original Use: Game retrieving, setting

Modern Use: Companion

Size: Height: 25–27 in.

Weight: 60–70 lb

Colors: Chestnut red

Recognized by: A.K.C., K.C.

Often called a red setter, the Irish setter was also once called a 'red spaniel', and is one of the most popular breeds of setters – much more widely known than its cousins the Irish red-and-white setter (see page 61) and the English setter. The red setter is undoubtedly a good–looking and affectionate dog, but they can also be very exuberant and love nothing more than galloping through fields and parks – especially with other dogs!

In common with most other Irish breeds, the exact origins of the Irish setter are uncertain: it is possible that the Old Spanish pointer, a breed unknown outside of Spain, setting spaniels and early Scottish setters may have been contributed to the development of the breed which is known to have existed in the early 18th century and was used by the Irish landed gentry to find game on their estates.

Today Irish setters still have a 'good nose' but few are used for working because the breed has unfortunately gained a – largely undeserved – reputation for being 'flighty' and 'excitable', which lead them to be unpredictable in the field. Like its red-and-white cousin, the Irish setter takes more time to obedience-train than other gun dogs. This is because as a breed, they are late to mature – they retain their youthful 'joie de vivre' for much longer! But, once trained, they do indeed make very reliable companions.

The breed standard for these gorgeous, gregarious dogs calls for a 'racey' dog, with a kind expression in the oval-shaped eyes, and the rich, glowing, chestnut-red coat, which is silky and flat to the body but abundantly feathered at the top of the ears, on the legs and the tail. The sensitive nose is usually black or a lovely chocolate color.

Irish Red-and-White Setter

Other Names: **Parti-colored Setter**
Date of Origin: **18th century**
Place of Origin: **Ireland**
Original Use: **Setting, game retrieving**
Modern Use: **Gun dog, companion**
Size: Height: **23–27 in.**
      Weight: **60–70 lb**
Colors: **Red-white**
Recognized by: **K.C.**

As with most Irish breeds, very little is known of their exact origins. We know that setters existed in the 18th century in Ireland, where they were used by the landed gentry to find game on their large estates. It may be possible that the evolved through some crosses with the Irish water spaniels, English setters (see page 56), Gordon setters (see page 58), springer spaniels and pointers.

Most people, when they think of Irish setters, remember first the 'modder rhu' or 'red dog' as it is called in Gaelic, the whole-colored, red Irish setter. A century ago, working Irish setters were not always red though; in fact, they were more often chestnut and white, or red and white. The breeders began to concentrate on the red-and-white variety. In Dublin before 1877,

Irish Setter classes were divided by color and the red-and-whites were in the majority. In the 20th century, the breed came close to extinction before being revived as a separate breed.

The Irish red-and-white setter is a little less tall than its red cousin and its deep chest, makes the breed prone to gastric torsion, commonly called 'bloat'. This is a sudden, painful and, sometimes, fatal disease where the stomach has become twisted, trapping gas, which then causes the abdomen to bloat. Surgical intervention is vital to save the dog. Like its redheaded cousin, the Irish red-and-white setter is exuberant, extrovert and enthusiastic with a highly refined sense of smell, but this character does mean that it takes more time to obedience-train than other gun dogs.

Pointer

Other Names: English pointer
Date of Origin: 17th century
Place of Origin: Great Britain
Original Use: Tracking game
Modern Use: Gun dog, companion
Size: Height: 24–27 in.
Weight: 44–66 lb
Colors: Black-white, liver-white, lemon-white, orange-white
Recognized by: A.K.C., K.C.

It is likely that the name of this breed started out as a general description: 'pointing dogs', which described the dog's work and gradually became shortened and then a proper name, 'pointer'. Its work was to find game in open country, which it did with its nose, and when it found it, the dog froze in the classic pose: nose held high, one foreleg lifted and bent, the tail held still, straight out, and level with the back. While it is believed the pointer came to England from Spain in the 18th century (where it had been developed in the 16th century), such dogs also existed in many European countries and in slightly differing forms: The Netherlands (once a Spanish dominion), France, Germany, and Denmark all had their own variations to suit the regions in which the dogs worked. The pointer – in this instance the name refers to the breed developed wholly in Great Britain – is a dog with an excellent nose, but a slow, ponderous nature. This speed was ideally suited to huntsmen armed with the early, muzzle-loading guns. Later technological developments improved the guns, which meant that instead of having to shoot

at birds while they roosted, flying birds could now be accurately targeted. Consequently, faster and more skillful gun dogs were required.

To make the pointer more robust, and to give it more speed, early breeders made crosses with foxhounds (see page 112): this nearly proved disastrous, since hounds work with their noses to the ground and their instinct is to chase and kill the quarry, while the pointer scents the air, stalks its prey but holds back from the kill. The offspring of these crosses tended to inherit the hounds 'skills'. Breeders tried again, this time it is suggested they used bulldogs, greyhounds, and bloodhounds and, chances are, the offspring of these crosses were even more 'useless' as pointers! It

was actually the dog show that rescued the breed from more 'tinkering': the first dog show in Newcastle, England, in 1859 was less a 'show' or exhibition, and more a competition, especially among the shooting men who argued incessantly over which dogs were the not only the finest gun dogs, but which were also the most 'handsome'. The show excited such interest that 'pointer men' now strove to breed a dog with the purest of forms, the result of which can be seen today. Even though few pointers are worked today, their good looks, and calm characters, which have made them firm favorites in many homes as loving pets, will surely ensure that the pointer will never disappear.

German Pointer (short-haired)

Other Names: **Deutscher Vorstehhund**
Date of Origin: **19th century**
Place of Origin: **Germany**
Original Use: **General hunting**
Modern Use: **Gun dog, companion**
Size: Height: **24–26 in.**
       Weight: **60–70 lb**
Colors: **Liver, liver-white, black-white, black**
Recognized by: **A.K.C., K.C.**

German pointers are a diverse group of breeds, with a variety of origins, and the result of intense breeding activity which took place in Germany in the late 19th century. The most well-known German pointers are the German short-haired pointer, the German wire-haired pointer, and the Weimaraner (see page 68), which are recognized by the American Kennel Club. There are, however, other less well know German pointers such as the German long-haired pointer (see page 66) and the Pudelpointer, both of which are recognized by the F.C.I. but not by the A.K.C.

The 'native' German pointers were heavy, slow, dogs and as with so many breeds, the German short-haired pointer was developed in the period from 1860 to 1880 when the Germans

were searching for an 'improved' all–purpose hunting dog. To achieve this, dogs of Spanish pointer origins were crossed with St. Hubert Hounds. This at least gave the dogs an excellent trailing nose.

One early breeder was Prince Albrecht zu Solms-Bauenfels of the House of Hanover, who, in 1870, laid down the dictum that the dog's form should follow its function and ability. Subsequently, Christian Bode of Altenau is said to have introduced English pointer blood to give the German dogs a greater wind-scenting nose and a more 'stylish', lean, and athletic appearance. In 1883, the foundations of the breed were established by two dogs, Nero and Treff, who tied for the German Derby that year.

The German short-haired pointer made its first appearance in Britain in 1887, but it would not be until 1950 that a breed club was established in the U.K.

Nevertheless, the German short-haired pointer became a great favorite with weekend hunters in Germany and in America, where it was introduced in 1925 by Dr. Charles R. Thornton of Missoula, Montana. Soon afterwards a breed club was established in the U.S.A. and' in 1930, the breed was admitted to the American Kennel Club.

The German wire-haired pointer, known in its homeland as the Deutscher Drahthaariger, was developed by crossing the offspring of German short-haired pointers with a number of other breeds including the wire-haired pointing griffon, the Pudelpointer and the Stichelhaar (broken-coated pointer). This produced another all-purpose dog, which could work on land and in water, flushing, pointing and retrieving.

German Pointer (long-haired)

Other Names: **Deutscher Vorstehhund**
Date of Origin: **19th century**
Place of Origin: **Germany**
Original Use: **General hunting**
Modern Use: **Gun dog, companion**
Size: Height: **24–26 in.**
        Weight: **60–70 lb**
Colors: **Red-and-black**
Recognized by: **F.C.I.**

One of the three distinct German pointer breeds developed in the late 19th century using 'native' stock and imported breeds, the German long-haired pointer is not well known outside of homeland, where it is primarily still a working dog, and it is recognized only by the F.C.I.

The breed made its first appearance in Hanover, Germany in 1879 and is the result of crossings of pointers with long-haired continental bird dogs such as the epagneul Français (French spaniel) (which gives the long-haired pointer its 'spaniel-like' looks and temperament), along with Irish and Gordon setters (see page 58) which produced the black-and-white coloration, although this is not generally accepted for registration. As with the other German pointers developed at the end of the 19th century, the aim was to produce a hunting dog that was lighter, faster, and keener than the existing pointers in Germany.

An attractive dog with long straight, legs delightfully fringed with soft hair, broad-based ears covered in wavy hair, and a gentle expression in the eyes, the German long-haired pointer also makes an excellent companion dog and a very good watchdog. Such attributes will no doubt ensure its continued existence and perhaps, greater notice outside of Germany.

Munsterlander (large)

The black-and-white colored Large Münsterlander is an all–purpose gun dog with a superb nose for scents, that was developed in Germany in the 19th century. While its ancestors were among the various German bird dogs, the Large Münsterlander breed really began as the black-and-white variation of the red-and-white German long-haired pointer (see page 66). When the German long-haired pointer declined in numbers, a breed was established for it and adopted, as its standard, only red-and-white specimens. Black-and-white puppies, however, continued to appear in litters and hunters in the Münster region of Germany, who were interested in the form and function of hunting dogs, began to breed from the black-and-white dogs. They subsequently formed a breed club in 1919 in order to

Other Names: **Grosser Münsterlander Vorstehhund**
Date of Origin: **19th century**
Place of Origin: **Germany**
Original Use: **Tracking, pointing, retrieving**
Modern Use: **Gun dog, companion**
Size: Height: **23–24 in.**
　　　Weight: **55–65 lb**
Colors: **Black-white**
Recognized by: **K.C.**

differentiate their animals from its smaller relative, the kleiner Münsterlander (small Münsterlander, also known as the Heidewachtel and the Spion) which is recognized only by the F.C.I.

The large Münsterlander is reputed to be the ideal gun dog for the 'rough shoot' and it is very enthusiastic in the field. In Germany, the dog is still used to hunt hare, fox and roe deer, and it works equally well on land and in water. In France, the Large Münsterlander is best known in the show ring, while in Britain the breed is now of interest to owners keen on maintaining the Münsterlander's working qualities.

Weimarana

Other Names: **Weimarana Vorstehhund (Weimar Pointer)**

Date of Origin: **17th century, but developed in early 19th century into modern form**

Place of Origin: **Germany**

Original Use: **Large game tracking**

Modern Use: **Gun dog, companion**

Size: Height: **22–27 in.**

Weight: **70–86 lb**

Colors: **Gray**

Recognized by: **A.K.C., K.C.**

A painting by the artist Anthony van Dyke (1599–1641) provides one of the earliest records of this uniquely colored breed. There is no other evidence to indicate the origins of the Weimarana but most assume that it is the result of crosses between the St. Hubert hound, bloodhounds (see page 107), and pointers. However, by the early 19th century, a distinctly gray-colored hunting dog was evident in Germany, and credit for developing and popularizing the breed is generally given to Grand Duke Karl August of Weimar, the capital of Thuringia. The Grand Duke's work was carried on by enthusiastic sportsmen keen on producing an 'all–purpose' hunting dog

that would not only enter water to retrieve fowl, but to blend the abilities of the tracking dogs with those of the pointers. The result was the gorgeous Weimarana, rippling with muscles – but also available in the lesser known long-haired variety.

The Weimarana was recognized in Germany as a distinct breed in 1896 and the following years, owners met at Erfort to form a breed club – not to popularize the breed though, but to save it from extinction by enforcing strict breeding rules with which owners had to abide. In 1943, the breed was recognized in the U.S.A. where it has grown steadily in popularity. While the Weimarana has proven itself more than proficient in field trials and obedience work, as a hunting dog and as a watchdog, it is undoubtedly its appearance that has captured most people's hearts: the shimmering gray coat – which earned it its nickname of 'Gray Ghost' – coupled with distinctive and arresting eyes ranging from amber, through gray to blue and physical grace, make the Weimarana a universally admired breed.

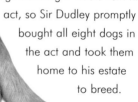

Golden Retriever

Other Names: **None**
Date of Origin: **19th century**
Place of Origin: **Great Britain**
Original Use: **Retrieving game**
Modern Use: **Gun dog, companion, guide dog for the blind**
Size: Height: **20–24 in.**
   Weight: **(6–8 lb)**
Colors: **Cream, gold**
Recognized by: **A.K.C., K.C.**

Quite possibly, the golden retriever is the most benign, good-natured, easiest to train – and the most willing to learn – breed of all dogs. A brilliant gun dog, wonderful family pet, and excellent guide dog for the blind, it is also one of the most popular breeds today. In the late 19th and early 20th centuries, the popular account of the breed's origins was based on a rather 'tall story', according to which, in 1858, Sir Dudley Majorbanks, while visiting the circus in Brighton, saw a troop of trained Russian sheepdogs perform. Sir Dudley was so impressed by their tricks and beauty that he wanted to have a pair immediately himself. The trainer of the dog troupe refused to sell two dogs claiming it would ruin his act, so Sir Dudley promptly bought all eight dogs in the act and took them home to his estate to breed.

The public 'lapped up' the story, but if these dogs were in fact herding dogs or 'sheepdogs', they would not make good retrievers: sheepdogs round up and hustle their charges along – and are not adverse to nipping the heels of slow movers to hurry them – while gun dogs must work in exactly the opposite manner: finding the object of interest with as little fuss as possible and taking it in their mouths without marking or damaging it any further. In the end, the mystery was solved when Sir Dudley's kennel records from 1835 to 1890 were published: Majorbanks had been breeding from 'sports' – animals which deviate slightly from the expected norm – and the original animal of the golden retriever breed was called Nous, a yellow dog bred from black, flat-coated retriever (see page 72) parents. Nous was mated with a small liver-coated tweed water spaniel (itself a small retriever), and the result was four golden retriever puppies, called

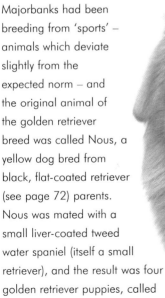

delightfully, Crocus, Ada, Primrose and Cowslip. Not a hint of Russian sheepdog in them! Instead the golden retriever was a 100% gun dog.

Since its introduction, four breed lines have been established: one continues to produce working gun dogs, the second line was developed for field trials, the third line (the largest) is for show dogs and family pets, while the fourth line produces dogs bred exclusively for training as assistants to blind and disabled people.

Flat-coated Retriever

Other Names: Originally called 'wavy-coated retriever'
Date of Origin: 19th century
Place of Origin: Great Britain
Original Use: Retrieving game
Modern Use: Gun dog, companion
Size: Height: 22–24 in.
      Weight: 60–89 lb
Colors: Liver, black
Recognized by: A.K.C., K.C.

Once game birds have been shot, they must be found. 'Springing' dogs, whose job it was to 'spring' the birds into the air, as well as most setters and pointers, were to the greater extent, uninterested in retrieving game for their masters. What was needed was a dog who would concentrate just on this task, and the early candidate was the flat-coated retriever, known originally as the wavy-coated retriever.

The first 'representative' of the breed to be seen in England was a dog called Wyndham, which was shown in Birmingham in 1860, and who aroused a great deal of interest among huntsmen, but from whose owner very little information about the breed could be gleaned. In the end it was concluded that the foundation stock for the breed came from smaller working dogs from the St. Johns region of Newfoundland. These dogs had come to Britain on fishing boats and were possibly used as guard dogs, but game keepers in the late 19th century were soon to discover their special talents and, following further crossings with setters (which 'flattened' out the wavy coat), the sleek, flat-coated retriever was soon a favorite gun dog. The arrival on the scene of the Labrador retriever and the golden retriever however, meant that by the end of World War II, the flat-coated variety was almost extinct. In the 1960s this handsome breed was rescued once more to become a much sought-after gun dog, whose numbers are sure to increase in line with its growing popularity as a companion dog.

Labrador Retriever

Other Names: **Labrador, small water dog**
Date of Origin: **19th century**
Place of Origin: **Great Britain**
Original Use: **Gun dog**
Modern Use: **Gun dog, field trails, companion,
    guiding/assistance dog**
Size: Height: **21½–22½ in.**
    Weight: **55–75 lb**
Colors: **Yellow, black, mid-brown**
Recognized by: **A.K.C., K.C.**

One of the world's most popular breeds, the waterproof, and water-loving Labrador was in first used in its native Newfoundland, Canada, a natural-born retriever – though not of birds! Their task was to go over the side of the fishing boats and drag the ends of the nets full of fish to the shore where they could be hauled up: the rocky inlets of the Labrador coast made it dangerous for fishing boats to approach the shores too closely. Once this task was done, the Labrador swam back to the boat, retrieving any objects lost overboard in the process. When the St. John's fishermen sailed to British ports to sell the catch, their dogs went with them and some remained in that country. In their native land, these

Labradors were called 'small water dogs' in order to distinguish them from the giant Newfoundland (see page 229) also found in the region. An early owner was the Earl of Malmesbury who wrote in a letter of 1879 that he had acquired such dogs from a Newfoundland fisherman in Poole, Dorset. The earl began breeding the dogs for use as gun dogs and wrote that he always called them 'Labradors' and the name has stuck firm ever since.

While still widely used as gun dogs, retrieving game on shoots, the Labrador, being among the most affable breeds, has found many a home as a loving and well loved pet. Regrettably, some dogs suffer from hereditary cataracts and hip and elbow arthritis. As they get older, they are also prone to weight gain, which can exacerbate any underlying joint problems.

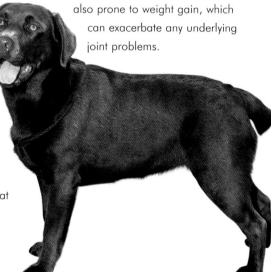

Curly-coated Retriever

The origins of this breed lie in the lesser Newfoundland dog – the 'small water dog' (see Labrador retriever, page 74) brought to England by the cod fishermen of St. John's, Newfoundland in the late 18th and 19th centuries, and the now extinct old water dog or English water spaniel. It also seems likely that further crosses with poodles (see page 194) were made, which would have improved the retrieving skills, though not the coat!

The curly-coated retriever is the largest, oldest (early evidence suggests that it existed as early as 1803) and the least well known of the British retrievers. It is distinguished by it marvellous coat of crisp, tight, and extremely waterproof curls. The result looks more like the finest astrakhan rather than dog, and can be either jet black or liver in color. One good shake is all it takes to get the coat almost completely dry. This is useful, for the curly-coated retriever delights in swimming and

Other Names: **None**
Date of Origin: **19th century**
Place of Origin: **Great Britain**
Original Use: **Retrieving waterfowl**
Modern Use: **Gun dog, companion**
Size: Height: **25–27 in.**
Weight: **70–80 lb**
Colors: **Black, liver**
Recognized by: **A.K.C., K.C.**

earned its place in the hearts of many 19th-century game keepers for its robust character and willingness to cross marshes, rivers and streams. The curly's kind and playful nature also made it a firm favorite among families with children.

In 1896 a club was formed to promote the breed and, for a while, the curly prospered – in the field, in the show ring, and in the home. Its heyday was undoubtedly during the interwar period (1918–1939) but the breed was soon eclipsed in popularity by its 'cousins' the Labrador retriever (see page 74) and the golden retriever (see page 70). In recent years interest in the breed has been revived and soon, no doubt, this calm, even-tempered, and delightful-looking breed will become firmly established in the hearts of many admirers once more.

Hungarian Vizsla

Elegant and energetic, the vizsla is Hungary's most famous native hunting dog. The name was first used in 1510 to describe the result of a crossing between the now extinct native pannonian hound with a yellow Turkish dog. It is more likely though that the breed is much more modern and its background may include Transylvanian pointing dogs and the Weimarana (see page 68) of Germany.

Other Names: Magyar vizsla, drotszoru Magyar vizsla, Hungarian yellow pointer
Date of Origin: Middle Ages (wire-haired version developed in 1930s)
Place of Origin: Hungary
Original Use: Hunting, falconry
Modern Use: Gun dog, companion
Size: Height: 22½ –25 in.
      Weight: 48½–66 lb
Colors: Solid colors ranging from rusty-gold to dark, sandy yellow (darker shades are preferred)
Recognized by: A.K.C., K.C.

Whatever its origins, by the 1850s the 'Hungarian yellow pointing dog' was well established and was widely employed as a dual purpose pointing and retrieving dog. In Hungary the dogs were trained to work close to the hunter on foot. While this meant that it was not as fast or wide ranging as a pointer, it was a very careful and diligent searcher, with fine scenting abilities for both tracking and airborne scents.

The beautiful vizsla owes its survival today to the concerted efforts of Hungarian expatriates who fled their homeland during World War II, taking their beloved dogs with them to new lives in other parts of Europe and North America. Since then the dual working purposes of the vizsla have been extended to include a third role, to which it is also ideally suited: as a steady, reliable, obedient, and well-loved family pet. Back home in Hungary, the breed has been revived once again as a working gun dog, while in

Canada, the wire-haired variety, developed in the 1930s, with its distinguishing 'old gentleman's whiskers', is a favorite among weekend hunters.

Bracco Italiano

Until very recently the powerfully built and unique-looking breed with its long bloodhound-like ears was extremely rare. It was rediscovered by Italian dog breeders and then by breeders elsewhere in Europe. Similar looking dogs had been extremely fashionable hunting dogs with the nobles at the Renaissance courts of Italy. The breed evolved in the northern regions of Italy, in Piedmont and Lombardy, where it proved to be a versatile hunter, capable of scenting, pointing and retrieving on both land and in water.

Its ancestry is largely unknown: some breeders claim that it was a result of crosses between the segugio (see page 120) and an ancient Asiatic mastiff.

Other Names: **Italian pointer, Italian setter**
Date of Origin: **18th century**
Place of Origin: **Italy**
Original Use: **Tracking, pointing, retrieving**
Modern Use: **Gun dog, companion**
Size: Height: **22–26½ in.**
    Weight: **55–88 lb**
Colors: **White, white-orange, white–chestnut**
Recognized by: **K.C.**

Others maintain that the bracco is descended from the St. Hubert hound – which would account for the ears!

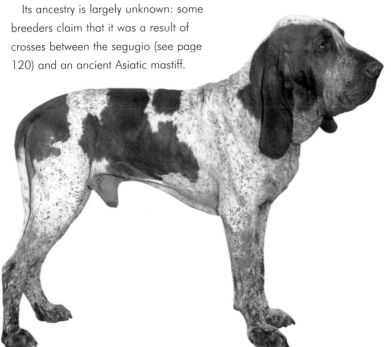

Italian Spinone

Other Names: **Spinone Italiano, spinone**
Date of Origin: **Middle Ages**
Place of Origin: **Italy**
Original Use: **Game retrieving**
Modern Use: **Gun dog, field trials, companion**
Size: Height: **24–26 in.**
     Weight: **71–82 lb**
Colors: **White, white-orange, white-chestnut**
Recognized by: **A.K.C., K.C.**

Like the Bracco Italiano (see page 79) the spinone developed in Piedmont and Lombardy in northern Italy. Although developed into its present form through selective breeding, the spinone is an ancient breed and is known to have existed – or at least varieties of the breed existed – in the 13th century. It is possible that it descended from the segugio (see page 120), while some claim descent from the ancient korthals griffon. In Italy the spinone is worked as a pointer, searching out and indicating the presence of game by the sudden freezing, the rigid posture, that makes the dog look as if it has turned to stone.

The spinone is a solid-looking dog, strongly boned, and well muscled, with a rather reserved look – largely due to its long whiskers. In character, the spinone thrives on work and is generally calm and easy going. But it can also be far from reserved and very playful – though its rather large size makes it a little clumsy! The spinone also has a tendency to dribble and drool somewhat,t and can have a rather pungent 'doggy' aroma. Fortunately these 'faults' are totally insufficient to detract from the positive attributes of this very obedient and happy breed: it has recently found great popularity beyond its native Italy in the U.S.A. and Canada, Scandinavia and Great Britain, as well as throughout the European Union countries.

Kooikerhondje

This breed is known to date back to the time of Dutch ruler, William of Orange (1650–1702) who, in 1688, became William III of England. Like the now-extinct English red decoy dog, the kooikerhondje assisted Dutch hunters by waving its bushy white tail around, and luring curious ducks and geese forwards into nets or traps made of rush matting. At one time, the waterfowl were netted for food, but today, the dogs assist in conservation programs where the ducks are leg-banded for identification.

During World War II, like many European breeds, the lovely kooikerhondje seriously declined in numbers and virtually disappeared: only 25 of the dogs survived the war. This small number formed the stock from which Baroness van Hardenbroek van Amerstool worked to recreate the breed. While, today, numbers are increasing, such a small gene pool does mean that inherited diseases do occur.

The kooiker's body is covered with a heavy, luxurious top coat of waterproof hair which conceals layers of insulating down. Most distinctive, however, are the ears with their dark, black 'ear–drops' of long hair.

Other Names: Kooiker dog, Dutch decoy spaniel
Date of Origin: 18th century
Place of Origin: The Netherlands
Original Use: Bird flushing and retrieving
Modern Use: Gun dog, companion
Size: Height: 14–16 in.
Weight: 20–24 lb
Colors: Red-white
Recognized by: K.C.

Portuguese Water Dog

Other Names: **Cao de Agua**
Date of Origin: **Middle Ages**
Place of Origin: **Portugal**
Original Use: **Fishermen's dogs**
Modern Use: **Retrieving, guarding, companion**
Size: Height: **17–22½ in.**
 Weight: **35–55 lb**
Colors: **Black, brown, white, black-white, brown-white**
Recognized by: **A.K.C., K.C.**

Found principally today in the Algarve region of Portugal, this ancient breed was used by Portuguese fishermen to help pull nets in the water, and as 'couriers' or message bearers, between boats. Meanwhile, on land, they also proved to be adept rabbiters. The cao de agua ('water dog') is said by many to have come originally from the Middle East, in the 700s with the Moors from North Africa. Others maintain that the breed arrived even earlier, in the 400s with the invading Visigoths before spreading through Europe to (possibly) produce both the poodle (see page 194) and the Irish

water spaniel.

Loyal, very strong, intelligent, and willing to learn, the cao de agua has two types of coats: it can be either long and wavy, or short and curly. Both coats were originally cut in a very distinctive way in order to stop the hind legs becoming 'waterlogged' and causing the dog to drag its legs and tire. The coat on the chest, belly and front legs was left longer to protect the dog from the shock of plunging into the cold Atlantic waters on the coast of Portugal. The delightful tail, which has a plume of hair left at the end which allows it to float, forms a ring when the dog is attentive.

BEAGLE

Hounds

The hound group of dogs includes various breeds which, for centuries, all over the world, helped man to hunt – for food and for sport. The hounds divide roughly into two groups: those like the greyhound and Afghan which hunt by sight, and pursue their quarry with great speed and agility, and, those like the basset hound and beagle which use their noses and great stamina to wear down their prey. Both types of hound do use all their senses when hunting but, while the scent hound will bark and howl when it encounters the scent of its quarry, the sight hound will chase silently.

There is a third group of dogs known as 'primitive dogs': these are descended from the Indian Plains wolf, *Canis lupus*

pallipes and genuinely 'primitive' dogs such as the Australian dingo, the New Guinea singing dog, and dogs such as the basenji, Canaan, Ibizan and pharaoh hounds, which share the same ancestry but have been 'developed' through breeding programs.

The sight, or gaze hound, is the product of selective breeding which began thousands of years ago. Arabia is the

CANAAN

original homeland of the Saluki and sloughi where, 5,000 years ago, they were bred to outrun the swift desert gazelles. Around 3,000 years ago, the ancient Egyptian were depicting greyhound-type dogs in their art.

AFGHAN HOUND

SLOUGHI

Sight hounds were most likely introduced into southern Europe around the shores of the Mediterranean, and into North Africa by Phoenician traders, and it is thought that, around 2,500 years ago, these traders also introduced sight hounds to Great Britain, where they were further selectively bred and then crossed with mastiff breeds to produce the muscular and powerful sight hounds like the Irish wolfhound and the Scottish deerhound. Like their Middle Eastern relatives, these hounds have the same elegant carriage and noble bearing that made them the sight hounds of the 'aristocracy', the clan chiefs of Scotland and Ireland.

A certain coolness and aloofness are the hallmarks of sight hounds: they are neither 'bouncy' nor exuberantly affectionate. But, while most sight hounds are now kept as companions, they still have their instinct to chase other 'fur'! One of the problems of having a sight hound in the home is the need for free exercise in a safe place: as they are not readily obedient, they must be exercised in a well-fenced area. Because they are agile dogs who can – and do – both jump and dig, garden fences need to be at least 6 ft high, with an additional 1 ft buried in concrete at the base!

The scent hounds are heavier dogs with a 'lower build' and are not as speedy as sight hounds. They do, however, have wide nostrils for picking up scents, pendulous ears which circulate air currents that carry scents, and deep flews, pendulous upper lips, which also act as scent 'traps'.

Medieval France was the undoubted leader in developing scent hounds, and 1,000 dogs at a time often worked the parks and forests of France in the service of the king. The oldest breed of French scent hound is thought to be the Porcelaine, a descendant of the now extinct

IRISH WOLFHOUND

BLOODHOUND

Britain today, the term 'to harry' is used to mean 'to worry' or 'to harass'.

Used to working in packs, scent hounds are more often willing to live together than any other type of dog, but they are happiest when at 'work', even when it is snuffling around for the scent left by the paws of the last dog to visit the path! All scent hounds bay, bark or what is known in hunting circles as 'give tongue' in order to help its fellow pack members. While owners and enthusiasts speak of the sounds as 'music', your neighbors may not!

Montaimbeouf. For over 1,000 years, until the French Revolution in 1789, the abbots of the Benedictine monastery of St. Hubert (now in modern Belgium) annually gave the king of France six St. Hubert hounds: today the descendant of these dogs is the famous bloodhound, the world's largest scent hound. Some scent hounds were smooth-haired, others were wire-haired — the griffons. Some were bred with short legs — the bassets (from 'bas' meaning 'low') — so that hunters could accompany these less speedy dogs on foot rather than horseback. Other small scent hounds developed in France, called harriers, which is derived from the Norman-French word harier, meaning to hunt. In

GRIFFON

Basenji

Other Names: **Congo dog**
Date of Origin: **Antiquity**
Place of Origin: **Central Africa**
Original Use: **Hunting**
Modern Use: **Hunting, companion**
Size: Height: **16–17 in.**
      Weight: **21–24 lb**
Colors: **Black-white, tan-white, black**
Recognized by: **A.K.C., K.C.**

One of the more unusual hunting dogs, the basenji has a very long history. Similar dogs with erect ears and very tightly curled, ring tail were depicted in ancient Egyptian art. In the 19th century, British explorers 'discovered' similar dogs in the Congo basin where they were used by their owners to point, retrieve, drive game, and track wounded prey. The basenji has a number

of 'unique' features: they cannot bark, but like wolves, howl or 'yodel'. When tracking game they are completely silent. Because of their silence, owners attached little wooden bells to their necks to help find their dogs when they were busy in dense undergrowth. Unlike other dogs, which have two breeding cycles a year, the basenji (again like the wolf) has only one, and, they clean themselves all over with their paw rather like a cat!

The first basenjis arrived in Britain in 1895, where they were entered at Crufts as 'Congo dogs' and aroused great interest. It was not until 1937, however, that a successful breeding program was established in Britain, because many of the 'imports' died of distemper: coming from a country where the disease was unknown made them particularly vulnerable. Soon after, in the early 1940s, the basenji became successfully established in the U.S.A.

The lightly built basenji is perfectly designed for its warm native climate: the loose skin, covered by a short, silky textured coat, helps with heat tolerance, while the coat colors provide camouflage in the bush. The basenji also has a rather wrinkled forehead which gives the dog a quizzical expression. The ears are set high and forward, and are very mobile, alert to every sound, and the jaws are long, typical of the most ancient breeds of dogs. The muzzle tapers from the dark, almond-shaped eyes to the tip of the black nose, while the long legs allow the basenji to move freely, in a graceful movement, rather like a trotting horse.

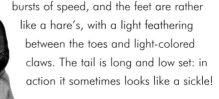

Ibizan Hound

Other Names: **Ca Eivissenc, Podenco Ibiceno, Balearic dog, Charnique (in France)**
Date of Origin: **Antiquity**
Place of Origin: **Balearic Islands, Spain**
Original Use: **Sight/scent/sound hound**
Modern Use: **Hunting/retrieving, companion**
Size: Height: **22–29 in.**
　　　 Weight: **42–55 lb**
Colors: **White, fawn, fawn-white, red, red-white**
Recognized by: **A.K.C., K.C.**

Hailing originally from Ibiza, in Spain's Balearic Islands – although now found also on the mainland and in France where it is known as the Charnique – three types of the strongly built Ibizan hound exist: smooth-haired, wire-haired and long-haired. Highly agile, the Ibizan hound can jump great heights without a 'take off' run! Incredibly versatile, these hounds hunt largely by scent and by sound, but do use sight as well, and will only bark when they sense their quarry. Furthermore, the Ibizan hound will hunt alone or work in a pack, and will both point and retrieve game.

The Ibizan hound has a long, narrow 'cone-shaped' head with a prominent occiputal bone and a lightly defined 'stop'. The length from the eyes to the point of the muzzle is always the same as from between the eyes to the occiput. The ears are pricked and can be turned forwards, horizontally sideways and backwards, and when the dog is alert, they are carried very high. The eyes are slanting and quite small, and a lovely amber color which matches the flesh-colored nose (which becomes lighter in color if the dog is unwell). The hind legs are strong and lean, well suited to bursts of speed, and the feet are rather like a hare's, with a light feathering between the toes and light-colored claws. The tail is long and low set: in action it sometimes looks like a sickle!

Pharaoh Hound

Other Names: **Kelb-tal kenek**
Date of Origin: **Antiquity**
Place of Origin: **Malta**
Original Use: **Sight/scent/sound hound**
Modern Use: **Hunting, companion**
Size: Height: **12–25 in.**
　　　Weight: **45–55 lb**
Colors: **Tan with white markings on extremities**
Recognized by: **A.K.C., K.C.**

Called *Kelb-tal Fenek* ('rabbit dog') on the island of Malta, from where it originates, the pharaoh dog only received this newer name when it reached the British show scenes in the 1960s because they bear a very strong resemblance to the hounds with large, erect ears seen in ancient Egyptian tomb paintings from around 4,000 BC. Furthermore, in the ancient Egyptian religion, the god Anubis was depicted with the head of an 'Egyptian hound', and so the name 'pharaoh hound' seemed highly appropriate.

This elegant, lithe hound, noted for its speed and agility, is probably descended from a small wolf, native to the Arabian Peninsula. The breed is thought to have been taken to the Mediterranean islands of Malta and neighbouring Gozo by Phoenician traders around 2,000 years

ago. Because of the isolated nature of the islands, the breed remained unadulterated and 'pure', and retains its ability to hunt by sight, sound, and scent.

A rich red color with white tips at the feet and tail, the coat is fine, gloss,y and short. Where white on the chest appears, a star-shape marking is preferred. The long, lean, chiselled head has powerful jaws, a nose that is flesh-colored (to blend with the coat and which becomes flushed when the hound is excited), oval, close-set amber eyes for excellent binocular vision to assist sight hunting, and high-set ears, broad at the base and fairly large, which are carried erect when the hound is alert. The tail is fairly thick at the base, but tapers to a point: when excited the tail may be carried high and circular, but it should never touch the back.

Afghan Hound

Other Names: Tazi, Baluchi hound
Date of Origin: Antiquity
Place of Origin: Afghanistan
Original Use: Large game hunting
Modern Use: Companion, guarding, hunting
Size: Height: 25–29 in.
      Weight: 50–60 lb
Colors: Any color
Recognized by: A.K.C., K.C.

The Afghan is a member of the greyhound family which first appeared in the eastern Mediterranean region several thousands of years ago, although it is not clear how it made its way from the Middle East to Afghanistan. Local legend says the hound was brought to Afghanistan in the Ark by Noah, but the most likely explanation is that it travelled with humans along the ancient trade routes, eventually to become the hunting dog of the Afghanistan royal family. Today, in Afghanistan, the hound exists in three varieties: short-haired (like the kyrghyz taigan, from Kyrgyzstan, the central Asian republic to the north of Afghanistan), fringe-haired (like the Saluki, see page 99), and the more familiar, long-haired dog, that we seen in the West.

The British Museum in London has in its collection a pictorial fabric from ancient Athens called *The Departure of Warriors* which is dated to around the 6th century BC. This picture shows a variety of greyhound with a 'feathered' tail and bears an uncanny resemblance to the Afghan hound. Another ancient source is a papyrus scroll from Sinai dating from around 3,000 BC which refers to a cynocephalus, which translates roughly as, 'a monkey– or, baboon-faced hound'. Wherever it actually originated, and however this magnificent animal came to be found in Afghanistan, when the first European explorers arrived in the country in the late 15th century, the Afghan hound was already there.

The remote nature of the country and the use of selective breeding modified the 'original' greyhound into a hound more suited to the climate and terrain of Afghanistan. In addition to the long, thick, warm, and protective coat, a distinctive feature is the feathered tail, carried high and ending in a circle or ring so the hunters could locate their dogs as they worked in the thick undergrowth. The Afghan's high and wide-set hipbones enables the dog to twist and turn on rocky hillsides and to leap like a monkey.

Highly prized by the Afghan nobility and aristocratic families, the hounds were difficult for 'mere foreigners' to obtain, and it was not until 1894 that the first Afghan hound reach Britain where its stunning appearance caused great interest. The hounds that followed over the next ten years or so, however, did not prove to be as 'interesting', and it may be that they were not pure-bred animals. Then, Captain Banff imported his Afghan hound called Zardin, which was shown at the K.C. show at the Crystal Palace in 1907: Zardin won in sensational style and was such a topic in the press that Queen Alexandra, the wife of King Edward VII, requested that Zardin attend a 'royal audience' at Buckingham Palace!

In conformation, their heads are long but not too narrow, with a slight stop (the indentation between the eyes where the nasal bone meets the skull) and long, strong jaws. The eyes are preferably dark, although sometimes they are a glorious golden color, and nearly 'triangular' in shape. The ears are set low and well back, close against the head. The back is level, but falls away slightly at the 'rump end' where the hips are wide and prominent and the hind legs powerful and with a good length between the hip and the hock. Thick hairs cover the large strong feet, ideally designed for rough terrain. The tail, which is lightly feathered and ends in the distinctive ring or circle, is set low when the hound is not in action, but raised high when the dog is running. The beautiful coat, which is acceptable in any color, is long and fine – and requires daily grooming to avoid thick mats – except on the 'saddle' from the shoulders backwards and on the fore face.

Borzoi

Other Names: **Russian wolfhound**
Date of Origin: **17th century**
Place of Origin: **Russia**
Original Use: **Wolf coursing**
Modern Use: **Companion**
Size: Height: **27–31 in.**
        Weight: **75–105 lb**
Colors: **Any color**
Recognized by: **A.K.C., K.C.**

The Russian word *borzoi* is a general term for sight hounds: the taigan, tasy, south Russian Steppe hound and chortaj are all classed as borzoi. Until fairly recently, the borzoi was known as the Russian wolfhound which, although a descriptive name, can be a little misleading. Pairs of borzoi were used in Imperial Russia for coursing wolves – a ceremonial kind of hunting and fashionable country pursuit among nobles. These dogs were never required to attack and fight wolves unaided, but 'to harry' wolves into open areas where human hunters could effect a kill more easily. The whole event was something of a spectacle, since symmetry and elegance in the paired dogs was highly valued, and both dogs were required to be matched in color and markings, as well as in size and speed, because one dog alone reaching and

harrying a wolf would not stand a chance! The two borzois' task was to seize the wolf by the neck and throw it to the ground, holding it there until the mounted hunter sprang from his horse and dispatched the unfortunate wolf in a suitably 'heroic' manner, with a dagger at close quarters.

The origins of the borzoi date back to the 17th century when a number of Arabian greyhounds similar to the Saluki (see page 99) were brought to Russia as hunting dogs. While they were fast, unfortunately their coats were not suited to withstand the severe cold of harsh Russian winters and they perished. When further greyhounds arrived, these were crossed with a native, long-legged collie-type dog which had a more suitable thick, heavy and wavy coat. The borzoi had arrived – in Russia at least. For the next 200 years the only borzois to leave Imperial Russia were those given as gifts to other royal households. In 1842, Queen Victoria was presented with the first of many borzois as gifts from the Russian Tsar. Victoria was immensely fond of the breed and as a 'fashion leader', she soon made the borzoi the 'most wanted' among the aristocracy of Britain. Early exhibitors of the breed at shows in the 19th century included the Duchess of Manchester, the

Duke of Hamilton, the Duchess of Newcastle, and King Edward VII and his wife Queen Alexandra. Around 1889, the Borzoi arrived in America: the first dogs came from England but, in 1903, Russian dogs, supplied by Grand Duke Nicholas Romanoff, arrived in the U.S.A..

The borzoi has an exceptionally long and lean head, measuring the same from the inner corner of the eye to both the nose and the occiput, with dark, almost almond-shaped eyes set obliquely and strong jaws. The body is best described as a series of graceful curves and, helping to give the borzoi its impression of streamlined strength, is well-muscled with, an arched back nearer the shoulders, powerful quarters that are set wider than the shoulders, and strong, well-muscled hind legs. The long, graceful almost hare-like feet – which some liken to the graceful arches of a Kirov ballerina – are covered in short, flat, hairs. The coat is long and silky, with a lovely frill on the neck, but short on the head, ears and front legs. The hind quarters and tail, on the other hand, are wonderfully 'feathered' so that even when still, the borzoi looks as if it is speeding through the wind!

Deerhound

Other Names: Scottish deerhound, Highland greyhound
Date of Origin: Middle Ages
Place of Origin: Great Britain
Original Use: Deer hunting
Modern Use: Companion
Size: Height: 28–30 in.
 Weight: 80–100 lb
Colors: Fawn, red, red-brindle, blue-gray, gray, black-brindle
Recognized by: A.K.C., K.C.

Once the exclusive companion to the kings and noblemen of Scotland in the Middle Ages – many were owned by the chiefs of Highland clans and for a time, men of rank lower than an earl were forbidden to own them – the deerhound is another descendant of the greyhound (see page 96). The exact date when these dogs reached the British Isles is unknown, but many believe it was first introduced by Phoenician traders around 3,000 years ago and then 'went north' to Scotland, where they proved to be of the greatest value, and where, possibly, they developed their heavy coats to withstand the tough Scottish climate.

The breed was developed to course deer through the densely wooded forests of the Scottish Highlands. During the 16th century, this was a favorite sport and pastime of the rich and powerful lairds, but when firearms became widespread in the 18th century, along with the clearing of much of the forests and the near collapse of the clan system following the Battle of Culloden in 1745, the favored position of the deerhound was ended. Thanks to the efforts of Duncan McNeil, later Lord Colonsay, who took a particular interest in the deerhound, the near-extinct breed was successfully brought back to enjoy true glory by a careful and systematic breeding program.

19th-century lovers of the breed included such notable figures as Queen Victoria and the great Scottish novelist, Sir Walter Scott, who had a monument erected to his deerhound, Maida, with the inscription: 'Beneath this sculptured form which late your wore, Sleep soundly, Maida, at your Master's door'. So beloved was his dog that he described him as 'the most perfect creature of heaven', and wrote of how, because Maida had so often had his portrait painted, he would get up and walk away whenever he saw anyone with a palette and brushes!

The deerhound looks very much like a greyhound, but with a very useful, weather-resistant coat! The hair on the body, neck and quarters is harsh and wiry, with a slight 'fringe' on the fore and hind legs. The head is broad at the ears and tapering to the nose, and is long and covered with quite long hair, with a lovely black nose – except in the blue-grays, where the nose is blue. One of the most endearing facial features is the 'moustache' of silky hairs,

which makes the deerhound look rather like a retired army colonel – very distinguished, rather formal, and perhaps a little forbidding! On closer inspection, however, one sees that the beautiful black-rimmed, dark brown eyes have the gentlest of expressions. The ears are set high on the head and when the deerhound is 'en repose' they are neatly folded. When aroused and excited by the prospect of a good run outdoors, the ears are raised expectantly. The long tail, which is thick at the root, tapers to the tip and should be long enough to almost reach the ground. The feet are remarkably compact for such a strong and agile dog, with only short hairs between the toes. Like all sight hounds, it is in action that the true form and beauty of the deerhound can best be appreciated.

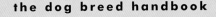

Greyhound

Other Names: **English greyhound**
Date of Origin: **Antiquity**
Place of Origin: **Egypt/ Middle East, but developed to present form in Great Britain**
Original Use: **Game coursing**
Modern Use: **Coursing, racing, companion**
Size: Height: **27–30 in.**
      Weight: **60–70 lb**
Colors: **White, fawn, red, red-brindle, black-brindle, black as well as any of the colors with white.**
Recognized by: **A.K.C., K.C.**

The earliest images of greyhounds appear in ancient Egyptian mural paintings. When the Romans invaded Egypt 2,000 years ago, similar dogs were spread around the Mediterranean, and around 400 BC the dogs arrived in Britain where they were developed to their present form. The origins of the name 'greyhound' is a matter of debate: some hold it is from 'grais' meaning 'Grecian; 'grei' the Anglo Saxon word for 'beautiful', 'grech' an old English word for 'dog', or even that is was a mispronunciation of the word 'gaze', descriptive of hounds which hunt by sight.

Whatever the origins of the name, for hundreds of years ownership of greyhounds in Britain was restricted to the nobility: in 1016 King Canute decreed that 'No mean (ordinary) person may keep any greyhounds'. Under King John, the penalty for killing a greyhound was the same as for murdering a man, and the exalted status of the hound is further evidenced by the king's willingness to accept greyhounds from nobles in lieu of taxes!

While the landowners of Britain made full use of the greyhound's hunting abilities, by the 18th century, the hound's sporting potential was also recognized and coursing grew in popularity. With a top speed of up to 37 mph greyhounds entered a new arena: racing. The first record of a race was in 1876 of a meeting held in Hendon, north London, but it did not seem to 'catch on'. It was in the United States that the sport developed: greyhound races appeared in 1890 in Miami as an added attraction at horse racing events. In 1909, in Tucson, Arizona the greyhound track in its modern form was born.

Irish Wolfhound

The Irish wolfhound is not only among the tallest breeds in the world, it is also one of the oldest. In AD 392, Symmachus wrote from Rome to his brother Flavinius, then in Britain, thanking him for the gift of seven Irish hounds and added that 'all Rome viewed them with wonder'. Not surprising given their great size! Throughout Irish history the wolfhound appears: King Cormac, who reigned in the 4th century, owned numerous wolfhounds; the 12th-century King of Ulster was so desperate to own a wolfhound called 'Aibe' that he offered six thousand cows for him and went into battle when the offer was declined! In the 16th century, a pair were sent to the King of Spain as a gift, but later, in 1652, Oliver Cromwell forbade their export because

Other Names: None
Date of Origin: Antiquity, but breed 'recreated' in 19th century
Place of Origin: Ireland
Original Use: Wolf hunting
Modern Use: Companion, guarding
Size: Height: 28–35 in.
        Weight: 90–120 lb
Colors: Variety
Recognized by: A.K.C., K.C.

97

the hounds were too rare and wolves were too plentiful! The last wolf to be killed in Ireland by the hounds was in 1780: their work was over and just 50 years later, it seemed the Irish wolfhound was extinct until English Army officer Captain G. A. Graham set about reviving the breed – although questions abound as to whether he found true Irish wolfhounds to breed from, or whether he 'manufactured' the breed from foreign breeds such as Great Danes (see page 216), deerhounds (see page 94) and mastiffs (see page 212).

In spite of their enormous size and strength, the Irish wolfhound is one of the gentlest breeds and is affectionate and loyal. It is only its size which makes it unsuitable for many homes, which generally lack the space needed to exercise such a magnificent animal. The head is long and not too broad, the muzzle long and moderately pointed. Underneath the shaggy brows are dark, soft, and good-natured eyes, shaded by black eyelids. The muscular thighs are long and strong, and the feet are large and round. The rough, topcoat is wiry on the body, legs and head, but longer over the eyes and under the jaws.

Saluki

Other Names: Gazelle hound, Arabian hound, Persian greyhound

Date of Origin: Antiquity

Place of Origin: Middle east

Original Use: Gazelle hunting

Modern Use: Companion, hare coursing (in countries where legally permitted)

Size: Height: 22–28 in.
      Weight: 31–55 lb

Colors: White, cream, red, golden, black-tan, fawn, tricolor

Recognized by: A.K.C., K.C.

The Saluki is a member of the greyhound family – one of the oldest families of dogs – and the Saluki may be the oldest member of this family! In the tomb of Rekma-re in Egypt, dating from around 1400 BC there is a painting of dogs that are remarkably 'Saluki-like', showing the same ear and leg feathering, similar hind quarters and tails. But even earlier paintings, such as those at Heirakonapolis dating from around 3600 BC, show similar dogs. According to legends, the Saluki takes its name either from the disappeared southern Arabian town of Saluk, once famous for its armor as well as its fine sight hounds, or from the town of Seleukia, in Syria. Its nickname of 'gazelle hound', however, indicates its original use and it was highly prized by the Arabs and Persians – as prized as their horses! It is said that, to protect their feet from the hot sands, Salukis were carried to the hunt on horse- or camel-back.

According to the tenets of Islam, dogs are considered as 'unclean' animals, but a special dispensation was accorded to the Saluki, which allowed them to share the living quarters of their owners. The nomadic Bedouin tribesmen of North Africa continue to hand down the genealogy of their prized Salukis as part of their oral tradition and continue to course game – although their dogs are more likely to be carried in four-wheel-drive vehicles!

The Saluki carries its head like a true aristocrat. The small, deep–set eyes have an expression described as 'far seeing' – indeed they will watch birds far in the distance, a legacy of their desert past when they hunted alongside hawks.

Sloughi

Other Names: **Slughi, sleughi, Arabian greyhound, eastern greyhound**

Date of Origin: **Antiquity**

Place of Origin: **North Africa, possibly Morocco.**

Original Use: **Hunting, guarding**

Modern Use: **Companion**

Size: Height: **24–28 in.**

Weight: **45–60 lb**

Colors: **'Sand' and fawn colors**

Recognized by: **K.C.**

Like the Saluki (see page 99) the sloughi, or Slughi, as it is called in colloquial Arabic, is a member of the greyhound family. At one time, the term greyhound was used as a 'catch all' name to describe a whole group of loosely related dogs, but when it became necessary to give individual names to the breeds, Britain, which was responsible for the naming process, decided that the term 'greyhound' should be applied to the short-coated 'English breed', and all others types – such as the Saluki, Afghan, and sloughi were to be known as Eastern greyhounds. Today, since many of the 'Eastern greyhounds' now have their own precise breed name, the term has largely fallen into disuse.

While the Saluki's origins are firmly rooted in the Middle East, the sloughi may have originated in the Yemeni town of Saloug and travelled into North Africa with the invading Arab tribes over 1,000 years ago, where it became established as a breed in Morocco. Like the Saluki, the sloughi was highly prized in a culture whose religion decreed dogs to be unclean: unlike 'ordinary' dogs, the sloughi shared their owners' homes and, it is said, were mourned as family when they died.

The sloughi is less well known than the Saluki, and is often confused with it. It is similar in size and shape to the Saluki, with a smooth, close coat designed to rid the body of excess desert heat. What the sloughi doesn't have are the Saluki's ear, leg and tail 'feathers'. The sloughi coat is also 'sand', 'biscuit' or fawn-colored – ideal camouflage for hunting desert prey such as gazelles, foxes, and hares. The sloughi's large ribcage gives the dog its vast lung capacity; the leg muscles, however, and the long, lean paws, are less developed and lighter than a greyhound's.

Whippet

While the names 'whappet' and 'wappet' are recorded in early English writings about dogs, these names, in fact, referred to any small – and noisy – dog of uncertain breeding. A 'miniature' greyhound, the perfect aerodynamic form of the whippet makes it a very fast mover, capable over short distances of reaching speeds of up to 40 mph. It is often called 'the poor man's greyhound,' perhaps because of the early edicts outlawing commoners from owning 'true' greyhounds in Britain, but more likely because these dogs were popular with working men in the north of England, who spent their weekend leisure time coursing rabbits. Terriers, the original breeds used for this 'sport' were not really fast enough to excel at the 'snap' (on the spot or hastily arranged) dog trials favored by the working classes, so careful crossing with small greyhounds began.

When anti-cruelty laws were introduced, owners turned to straight racing, training their dogs to run, grip and 'worry' a rag shaken by the owners. Rag racing required dogs with improved bodies and speed as well as a handicapping system: little dogs, the whippets, started at the front, bigger ones – greyhounds – at the rear! With purpose-built race tracks and commercial

Other Names: **Snap dog, 'Poor man's greyhound'**
Date of Origin: **19th century**
Place of Origin: **Great Britain**
Original Use: **Coursing, racing**
Modern Use: **Companion, racing**
Size: Height: **17–20 in.**
      Weight: **27–30 lb**
Colors: **Any**
Recognized by: **A.K.C., K.C.**

backing for greyhound racing in the 20th century, rag racing for whippets all but ended. Racing was revived as an amateur sport in the 1950s, using miniature starting traps – but no betting is allowed! Furthermore, unlike the divisions of greyhound 'type', a whippet can win in the show ring on one day, and the next day, be a winner at the races!

The immense power and speed of the whippet is more remarkable given the dog's outward appearance of great fragility, which is further enhanced by their habit of 'quivering' or 'shivering' when standing still and regarding you with quiet eyes! The truth is that the whippet is incredibly robust and has a supreme disregard for bad weather, and is so fearless that many suspect it to have the heart of a lion!

Basset Hound

Other Names: **None**
Date of Origin: **16th century**
Place of Origin: **France**
Original Use: **Rabbit/hare hunting**
Modern Use: **Companion**
Size: Height: **13–15 in.**
     Weight: **40–60 lb**
Colors: **Tricolor, lemon–white**
Recognized by: **A.K.C., K.C.**

The basset takes its name from the French word basset which means 'dwarf', and this breed of dog originated in France in the 16th century. The short-legged hunting hounds are distinguished not only by their lowness to the ground, but also by the remarkable scenting skill. The pendulous ears – which should reach at least to the end of the muzzle – may well have been useful for directing scents: as they flapped and brushed against the undergrowth, they circulated currents of air carrying the scent of quarry to their noses.

Today, the breed is considered a gentle and benign creature – if often a little obstinate – and worldwide they are famous as the symbol of the comfortable, well-fitting shoes! However, some lighter-boned, slightly longer-legged bassets do take part in field trials, displaying the skills that made them prized as hunting dogs for centuries.

The typical pet basset, however, is more likely to be the heavily boned dog on short, rather crooked legs. Weighing an average of about 55 lb, and coming in at under 15 in., basset hounds may be low-slung, but they are certainly not small dogs! The wrinkled skin, heavy flews, floppy ears, and soft, slightly sunken eyes (which give the basset a rather doleful expression) are also misleading, for they are playful dogs, with hearty appetites for food and exercise!

103

Grand Basset Griffon Vendéen

Other Names: Large Vendéen griffon basset
Date of Origin: 19th century
Place of Origin: France
Original Use: Gun dog, hare coursing
Modern Use: Companion, gun dog (in France)
Size: Height: 15–16 in.
Weight: 40–44 lb
Colors: White, gray, black-white, tan-white, tricolor
Recognized by: A.K.C., K.C.

The basset griffon Vendéen (from the Vendée region of France) comes in two sizes: *grand* (large) and *petit* (small) (see page 105). A scenting dog from the region, with the short (*bas*) legs that give the breed its name was known in the 19th century, but the modern grand basset griffon was established in the mid-1940s by selective breeding by Paul Desamy who fixed the characteristics of the breed. The grand basset griffon is a little taller and a little 'longer in the legs' than most bassets, and unlike the basset hound (see page 103) its conformation is less exaggerated,

the skin is not so wrinkled and it does not have the same 'serious expression'. The basset griffon's coat is also much harsher and shaggier! Like all bassets their pendulous ears – which should touch the end of their noses when scenting – help to circulate air currents carrying the scent of their quarry. They are also well-muscled dogs, with a heavy bone structure, which allows them the strength to be persistent – some would say obstinate – hunters.

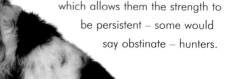

Petit Basset Griffon Vendéen

Like its 'big brother' the petit basset griffon has its origins in the Vendée region of France in the 18th century, where it was used for hunting rabbits and hares. In the 1940s, selective breeding by Abel Desamy fixed the breed's modern characteristics and helped to establish it as one of the most popular basset breeds – both inside France and abroad. The petit basset griffon is a more 'true' basset in shape: with the typical firm, short legs of the breed – although the front legs do not turn inward at the knees like the basset hound (see page 103). The petit shares the same deep chest as the grand basset: placed side by side the only discernible difference is in leg length: both have the shaggy coat, robust neck, and domed, elongated head. The shortened legs combined with the length of the back and the deep chest mean that the petit does have a tendency to suffer from back pain.

Other Names: Little griffon Vendéen basset
Date of Origin: 18th century
Place of Origin: France
Original Use: Hare coursing
Modern Use: Companion, gun dog (in France)
Size: Height: 13–15 in.
 Weight: 31–40 lb
Colors: White, orange-white, tricolor
Recognized by: A.K.C., K.C.

Beagle

Other Names: English beagle
Date of Origin: 11th century
Place of Origin: France, then developed in Great Britain
Original Use: Rabbit/hare hunting
Modern Use: Companion, gun dog, filed trials
Size: Height: 13–16 in
      Weight: 18–30 lb
Colors: Any hound color
Recognized by: A.K.C., K.C.

The beagle is the smallest of the British scent hounds, whose ancestors are believed to date back to the arrival of the Norman-French forces in Britain, led by William the Conqueror in the 11th century. As well as invading Britain, the Normans also introduced hares to the country to widen both the culinary (a pleasant change to the native rabbits) and sporting opportunities of the English!

The name 'beagle' may have originated in one of three sources: from the Celtic word 'beag', from the Norman-French word 'beigh' or from the Old English word 'begle', but all three mean the same thing: 'small'. In the late 18th century, beagles were often so small – under 10 in. that they were called 'pocket beagles' because the hunters could carry them in their saddle bags. The slightly larger sized 'modern' beagle was used almost exclusively as a working dog until the late 1940s in Britain, while in tropical countries, oversize beagles are still used in packs for hunting jaguars and leopards!

While the beagle may vary in size and looks from country to country – some have smooth coats, others can be wiry – one characteristic they all share is its' 'voice' – described as 'harmonious music' by enthusiasts – who listen for changes in 'song' if a rabbit – or dinner bowl – comes into view!

One of the saddest – and most controversial – roles of the beagle in recent years has been as a research dog in laboratories, both for medical research and commercial research. Because of their small size and uniformity in weight, large numbers of genetically bred beagles are produced specifically for this 'market'.

Bloodhound

The largest of the scent hounds, the bloodhound also has the keenest nose, able to detect the coldest of scents, and the unique ability to track people. While the movies depict a fearsome, drooling animal, baying after the scent of escaped criminals and ready to kill, in truth, the bloodhound lives only for tracking, with little or no interest in the 'end product'. Rather than bite their 'prey', bloodhounds are more

Other Names: Chien St. Hubert, St. Hubert hound
Date of Origin: Middle Ages
Place of Origin: Abbey of St. Hubert, Ardennes, Belgium
Original Use: Tracking ground scent of deer
Modern Use: Tracking, companion
Size: Height: 23–27 in.
Weight: 80–110 lb
Colors: Red, liver-tan, black-tan
Recognized by: A.K.C., K.C.

likely to slobber all over them! The use of the word 'blood' in their name refers not to their killing instinct, but to the fact that the hound was a member of an 'aristocracy' – rather like the way pedigree or thoroughbred horses are described.

The bloodhound traces its origins back to the Abbey of St. Hubert, which had been founded in AD 687 in the Ardennes, in Belgium, and where the monks bred these superb hounds for tracking deer. At the same time in Britain, identical hounds were being bred, most likely derived from the St. Hubert stock, but brought to England by nobles returning from the Crusades. At this time, these hounds occurred in a wide variety of solid colors, including white,

which was known as the talbot hound. Today, all bloodhounds are red, black and tan, or liver and tan. By the 17th century, the white strain had died out as a breed, but the gene continued and can be seen in white boxers and in tricolor basset hounds (see page 103).

Size and 'song' apart, a bloodhound's head is its most distinctive feature, with its abundance of loose skin which, when the dog lowers its head to scent, hangs in folds over its forehead and the sides of its face. The lower lips hang 2 in. below the jaw bone. The powerful neck and shoulders and the exceptionally strong back, allow the bloodhound to work for extended periods without rest.

Dachshund

The German name 'dachshund' translates as 'badger dog', which describes the dog's original role, in scenting and flushing out badgers which had 'gone to earth'. Its long, sausage-like body, short legs and rather big feet, allowed it to travel down narrow holes and tunnels and to dig out the quarry. Alternatively, the dachshund could hold a badger at bay in its earth, by barking continuously – its big ribcage gives this little dog a bark with tremendous resonance – until the badger was dug out with shovels. Technically then, the dachshund, is actually an 'earth dog', a terrier, but when the breed was first introduced to Britain by Prince Albert, the German husband of Queen Victoria, 'hund' was translated as 'hound' and the dachshund was placed in this group.

The dachshund today exists in six breeds: smooth-haired, long-haired and wire-haired, with miniature and standard varieties in each. The standard dachshunds – of all coats – vary in size. In Germany, where the dogs are still worked, they are categorized by their chest measurements:

Other Names: Kaninchenteckel (rabbit-hunting) Normalschlag (standard), Zwergteckel (miniature), 'sausage dog'
Date of Origin: 19th century
Place of Origin: Germany
Original Use: Badger flushing
Modern Use: Companion
Size: Height: Standard and miniature: 5–10 in.
Weight: Miniature: 9–10 lb
standard: 15–25 lb
Colors: Variety of colors, but white markings undesirable in show dogs
Recognized by: A.K.C., K.C.

Kaninchenteckel ('rabbit–hunting' dachshund) has a maximum of 12 in. chest circumference; *Zwergteckel* (miniature) measures 12–14 in.; *Normalschlag* (standard) measures over 14 inches.

While the smooth-haired standard dachshund, with its lustrous coat, is perhaps the oldest of the breed, the long-haired standard, with its silky-smooth, rather glamorous coat, seems to have been developed by crossing smooth-haired standards with short-legged spaniels such as the Sussex spaniel (see page 50) or field spaniel (see page 48). Miniature versions of each were then created. The wire-haired dachshund, with its thick and wiry, but flat, topcoat coupled with a fine undercoat, was the result of crossing the smooth-haired dachshund with wire-haired pinschers, with further crosses of the

offspring with Dandie Dinmont terriers (see page 129). Evidence of this ancestry can be seen in the way wire-haired dachshunds do not share the same 'tapering' nose of the other 'dachs' and it is further distinguished by the wiry 'beard' and bushy 'eyebrows'.

Elkhound

The elkhound – or more correctly, the Norwegian elkhound, the national dog of Norway – is a member of the spitz group of dogs that evolved in the Arctic regions of the world: Scandinavia, Canada, Russia, and Alaska. In conformation, spitz-type dogs are close to the northern wolf. The sharp, erect ears, the rather straight hocks, the lovely ruff around the neck and the tightly curled tail over their backs are the telltale signs of the elkhound's origins, and they are ,indeed, well suited to harsh northern climates. Spitz dogs have an insulating, water-resistant undercoat that is as dense as the top coat; the small ears reduce any heat loss and minimize the risk of frost bite, while thick fur grows between the toes to protect them on snow and ice.

Other Names: Norwegian Elkhound, Norsk Elghund (Gra) (Gray), grahund, Swedish Gray Dog
Date of Origin: Antiquity, show standards developed in 1879
Place of Origin: Norway
Original Use: Elk hunting
Modern Use: Companion, gun dog, search and rescue
Size: Height: 9–21 in.
    Weight: 44–50 lb
Colors: Varied shades of gray, with black tips to long outer coat, lighter on chest, neck, buttocks and underside of tail
Recognized by: A.K.C., K.C.

From Stone Age fossils found in Norway, it is evident that the breed has existed in Scandinavia for some 5,000 years and was originally bred for hunting elk (or moose). In Britain, the elkhound is classified in the hound group because it hunts by scent to locate the quarry before alerting the huntsman by barking. The hound holds the elk at bay by 'dancing' around and in front of it – for up to an hour – always dodging the elk's formidable hooves and antlers.

Today, the versatile elkhound can be found herding farmyard livestock, working as a gun dog and, increasingly – owing to their scenting skills – as mountain search-and-rescue dogs.

Foxhound

Other Names: **known in U.S.A. as 'English' foxhound to distinguish it from the 'American' foxhound**
Date of Origin: **13th century**
Place of Origin: **Great Britain**
Original Use: **Fox hunting**
Modern Use: **Fox hunting (in areas where still legal)**
Size: Height: **23–27 in.**
     Weight: **55–75 lb**
Colors: **Bicolor, tricolor**
Recognized by: **A.K.C., K.C.**

While never a pet – although they do make excellent companions – nor really a show dog, the foxhound is nevertheless, probably one of the most instantly recognized breeds, and one which is subject to a great deal of public debate with regard to the legislation of fox hunting in Britain. Organized fox hunting became established in Britain in the 13th century: prior to that it had simply been a method of culling vermin, with stag hunting the more fashionable sporting pursuit. The first objective in the new sport of fox hunting, was to produce a lighter and faster dog than the St. Hubert-type hounds (see bloodhound, page 107) then available for hunting.

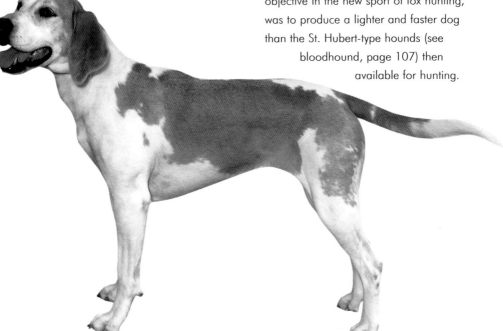

Imported French hounds, crossed with native animals, produced faster, leaner dogs, but each of the regions developed hounds that varied in shape and size: Yorkshire hounds were considered the fastest, while Staffordshire hounds were larger, a little slower but with a deeper voice. The differences were largely due to the types of terrain in which the hounds worked. In the 18th century, stag hunting declined and, by 1800, large, standardized packs of hounds were being bred and careful records were being kept that were incorporated into stud books kept by the Master of Foxhounds Association. These stud books provide valuable data and allow many packs to trace their hounds back over 200 years, making the English foxhound the oldest recorded pedigree. Years of selective breeding have produced an efficient hound, with a keen nose for scenting, a good voice, stamina – hunt distances of 50 miles are not unusual, with many hounds racing to the start under their own steam on their powerful legs and with great enthusiasm.

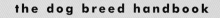

Finnish Spitz

Other Names: Suomenpystykorva, Finsk spets, barking bird dog
Date of Origin: Antiquity
Place of Origin: Finland
Original Use: Tracking animals – from bears to squirrels
Modern Use: Gun dog, guarding, companion
Size: Height: 15–20 in.
      Weight: 31–35 lb
Colors: Bright reddish-brown or yellowish-red, but lighter on cheeks, under muzzle, on breast, inside legs, at back of thighs and under tail
Recognized by: A.K.C., K.C.

The national breed of Finland, this is another spitz-type dog that has been around for thousands of years and, for centuries, inhabited the eastern part of Finland and the Karelian region of Russia (following the Russian Revolution in 1917, the hounds living in this region became known as Karelo-Finnish laikas). Legend says the ancestors of the Finnish spitz lived in the primeval forests where they helped the tribes or clans of Finns to track bears and elks. They have a particularly good nose for scent – which is why they are included in the hound group – but are also adept at listening to the forest floors for the sounds of animals and bird wings; they would force the animal out of cover to seek sanctuary in a tree. Then, using its bark to alert the hunter, the Finnish spitz would stand in rigid point marking the bird's or squirrel's position. This ability to track earned the spitz its nickname of the 'barking bird dog'.

By the 20th century, however, the breed had become repeatedly crossed with other Scandinavian spitz breeds and few pure specimens remained until expeditions to the far north of the country returned with magnificent animals with which the Finnish Kennel Club was able to begin a breed register and maintain detailed pedigrees.

These handsome hounds, popular in their native land and growing in popularity abroad, are distinguished by their bushy, bright red-gold coats (double for weatherproofing), which shade off into rich creamy fawn on the under parts and their curled tail held against the thigh.

Grand Bleu de Gascogne

The grand bleu de Gascogne is thought by many to be descended from racing breeds brought to France by Phoenician traders. While this cannot be proven, the grand bleu is certainly one of the world's oldest hounds. Developed in the Middle Ages in the arid Gascony region of southwest France to hunt large game, the breed is now popular outside France, especially in the United States where it has been bred since the 18th century. In most cases, the grand blue continues to be a scent-trailing working dog, even though wolves and wild boars may have declined in numbers!

Other Names: Large blue Gascony hound
Date of Origin: Middle Ages
Place of Origin: France
Original Use: Deer/boar/wolf hunting
Modern Use: Gun dog
Size: Height: 24–28 in.
        Weight: 71–77 lb
Colors: Blue
Recognized by: K.C.

The coat is fairly thick and quite long – designed to give protection from angry teeth, tusks, and horns. The forelegs are incredibly well-muscled and support exceptionally strong shoulders. The pendulous ears are quite distinctive, being very low set and slightly curled!

Through selective breeding of the grand bleu de Gascogne for reduction in size to hunt smaller quarry, the petit bleu de Gascogne (small blue Gascony hound) was also developed in the Middle Ages. This smaller hound has the same remarkable nose for scents as its 'big brother', but lacks the curled ears and usually has tan-colored feet.

115

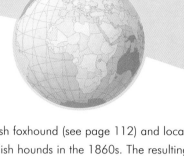

Hamiltonstovare

Other Names: **Hamilton hound**
Date of Origin: **Middle Ages, developed further in 19th century**
Place of Origin: **Sweden**
Original Use: **Hare and fox hunting**
Modern Use: **Hunting, companion**
Size: Height: **19–24 in.**
　　　Weight: **50–60 lb**
Colors: **Tricolor**
Recognized by: **K.C.**

The Hamiltonstovare is a Swedish hound named after the breed's creator, Adolf Patrick Hamilton, who was also the founder of the Swedish Kennel Club in 1889. The Hamiltonstovare was developed by crossing varieties of German beagle with the English foxhound (see page 112) and local Swedish hounds in the 1860s. The resulting Hamiltonstovare is a single, rather than pack hunter, capable of both scent-tracking and flushing game, while baying in a typically hound-ike manner when it finds its quarry.

The harsh climate and difficult terrain in which the hound has to work calls for a very hardy animal, with a strong dense topcoat covering a short, thick, yet soft undercoat to protect it from the cold, and, in winter, the Hamiltonstovare's coat also thickens very considerably .

While the breed remains little known outside of its native Sweden, the Hamiltonstovare is among the country's ten most populous breeds, where its attractive appearance – due to its calm brown eyes, long muzzle, tipped with a lovely large black nose, its striking tricoloration – and, most of all, its affectionate nature, have made the Hamiltonstovare both a magnificent show dog and a loyal companion dog. Without doubt, the Hamiltonstovare will become a firm favorite with dog lovers in many other countries too.

Otterhound

In Britain, different hounds were bred for different game: foxhounds for foxes, and harriers for hares, for example. It is possible that the otterhound is descended from the bloodhound (see page 107) – its 'nose' for scents is equal to that of a bloodhound – with some foxhound, spaniel, and large, rough-coated terrier (like the Airedale, see page 123) blood.

The otterhound was bred to swim in the coldest of rivers: it has a double coat with a thick, oily, woolly undercoat under coarse, outer hair that is also oily, insulating it from the iciest of water; its toes are webbed, and its legs are well-muscled for swimming – for hours at a time!

Other Names: **None**
Date of Origin: **Antiquity**
Place of Origin: **Great Britain**
Original Use: **Otter hunting**
Modern Use: **Companion**
Size: Height: **23–27 in.**
      Weight: **65–120 lb**
Colors: **Any hound colors**
Recognized by: **A.K.C., K.C.**

Otters live in holes dug underneath the banks of rivers with the entrance hole (the holt) under water. On land, the scent or trail left by an otter is called a 'drag', while scent left on water is called a 'wash'. The sensitive nose of the otterhound can follow a drag that is ten hours old. But otters, who swim for long distances under water, surface occasionally to take a breath. When they submerge again, the otter leaves behind a small trail of bubbles, marking its course. It is this trail (the wash) that the otterhound follows, swimming sometimes for up to five hours after its quarry.

Now that otters are no longer hunted, the otterhound's original function no longer applies. Fortunately, their lovely looks and even temperament have made them an attractive companion. They do have some drawbacks, though, as pets. Firstly, their absolute dedication to following and unravelling elusive scents on land makes them deaf to all commands! Secondly, they are irresistibly drawn by the sight or smell of water – no matter how deep or dirty – and they will paddle and swim around happily for hours, ignoring the requests of their owners to 'come out'. Thirdly, the oily nature of their coat, without frequent bathing or swims, makes the otterhound a rather pungent dog!

Rhodesian Ridgeback

Other Names: African Lion Hound
Date of Origin: 19th century
Place of Origin: South Africa
Original Use: Hunting
Modern Use: Companion, guard dog
Size: Height: 24–27 in.
Weight: 65–85 lb
Colors: Light-wheaten to red-wheaten
Recognized by: A.K.C., K.C.

Although it is true that this hound has a ridge along its back, it is not true that it 'originated' in Rhodesia (now modern Zimbabwe). The ancestors of this breed were a type of dog long used by the Hottentots of South Africa as guard dogs for their herds. A reddish-tan in color, they had a ridge of hair running down the spine, lying in the opposite direction to the rest of the coat – it runs towards the head, not away from it. They were, however, quite small dogs – until European settlers arrived in 1652 with their hounds and gun dogs. Many of the non-native dogs were unsuited to the rigors and diseases of their new home, so the tough native dog was crossed in to make the various imported dogs hardier – especially Dutch and German mastiffs. In the process, the small ridgebacked dog grew in size and developed a keen nose for scenting.

This was very fortuitous, since at the time, the Cape region of South Africa teemed with big game. Later, South African big-game hunters took the breed north to 'lion country' – to what was then Rhodesia. The ridgeback was never used to attack lions, but instead was expected to act like a true hound: scenting and trailing the game, barking to hold both the lion at bay and to attract the hunter's attention. For its defense, the ridgeback relied on its sheer size and strength as it snapped, dodged, feinted, and backed off to hold the lion's attention.

The breed was still somewhat 'rough and ready' until 1922 when an official standard was drawn up in Bulawayo, Rhodesia (Zimbabwe), combining the best attributes of five existing dogs. Few Rhodesian ridgebacks are worked today in big game tracking, instead serving as guard dogs on remote farmsteads.

119

Segugio Italiano

Other Names: Segugio, Italian hound
Date of Origin: Antiquity
Place of Origin: Italy
Original Use: Game hunting
Modern Use: Gun dog, companion
Size: Height: 20–23 in.
      Weight: 40–62 lb
Colors: Fawn, black-tan
Recognized by: A.K.C., K.C.

The segugio Italiano is Italy's only native scent hound and it is very similar to the coursing hounds seen in ancient Egyptian art, although its stamina was later greatly increased with the introduction of mastiff (see page 212) blood. Consequently the segugio has the long legs of a sight hound with the face of a scent hound! During the Renaissance in Italy, the segugio was highly prized – and is often to be seen in many paintings depicting hunting scenes at this time. Once it has a scent, the segugio is as single-minded in its determination to track as a bloodhound, but unlike that breed, the segugio is also very interested in the capture and kill of its quarry.

When not working, the segugio is a quiet and gentle dog, with an elegant outline, and a wonderful fawn, or black-and-tan coat which is dense and glossy. The tail is that of a sight hound – delicate and thin, even at the root – while the scent hound's pendulous triangular ears are set just below eye level and reach to the tip of the nose. The eyes themselves are large, dark, and bright, while the feet are oval in shape, rather like a hare's – which it still hunts today in its native Italy – and are covered in short, dense hair. The segugio is not normally used as a pack hound: more often it is worked singly or as a pair, finding, tracking and driving quarry towards waiting guns.

BEDLINGTON

Terriers

The majority of the world's terriers evolved in Britain from various hounds. The name 'terrier' is derived from the Latin 'terra', meaning 'earth', and the Roman invaders of Britain called these dogs 'terrarii' because they were expert tunnellers, willing to 'go to ground' after badgers, rats, rabbits, or foxes. In later centuries, terriers were associated, first, with the 'peasant classes' and then with the working classes of industrialized Britain. This is probably due to the fact that hounds and spaniels were the hunting dogs of the nobility – ancient laws in Britain and Ireland prohibited peasants from owning hunting dogs – and consequently, little reference is made of terriers until 1560 when Dr. John Caius remarked that terriers were quarrelsome, 'snappy' and fit only to live in stables!

Terriers were, nevertheless, valuable dogs in both countryside and towns for their efficiency as vermin 'killing machines' and also for sport. The Patterdale and Yorkshire Terriers were renowned for their ratting skills, and sport ratting – where the dogs were placed in pit and killed 'against the clock' – was popular across England and Ireland. In other regions, other terriers were developed to fight against each other, or other animals, in pits or in open fields.

STAFFORDSHIRE BULL

DANDIE DINMONT

Dogs used for bull baiting were large mastiff-type animals with added terrier blood to give them the edge when it came to fearlessness and aggression: the American pit bull terrier, Staffordshire bull terrier, and English bull terrier were all produced as a result of this 'sport'. The 'lamb-like' Bedlington terrier is the only racing terrier – said to be descended from whippets – and was bred by gypsies in the Rothbury Forest on the Scottish border!

In the 19th century, breeders seriously began breeding to type and produced the numerous regional variations: in Scotland, the generic, short-legged dogs became the Skye and Scottish terriers, Sealyham, cairn Terriers – the white-colored dogs becoming the West Highland whites – and the delightfully named, though utterly fearless, Dandie Dinmont.

Similar developments occurred across England, Wales, and Ireland so that, today, there are 29 British breeds of terrier, as well as European, Japanese, Russian, and Australian terriers. While they continue to retain their independent, tenacious characters and, if truth be told, remain completely convinced of their own 'self importance', terriers do make wonderful companions and pets.

CAIRN

HIGHLAND WESTIE

Airedale

The 'king of terriers', the Airedale, is the largest of the terriers, and is, in fact, too large to 'go to earth'. The Airedale, from the district in Yorkshire of the same name is thought to be a 'mixture' of otterhound (see page 117), and the now extinct 'black-and-tan' or old English broken-haired terrier. While other terriers were deliberately bred to reduce them in size, the Airedale was encouraged to grow in order to produce a dog that would take on an adult badger or otter. Its ancestry in the otterhound gave it both size, and its notably water skills, which earned it the nick name 'waterside terrier'. The Airedale, in true terrier style, also excelled at rabbit and rat hunting.

In 1879 the breed was officially classified at a dog show – in Bingley,

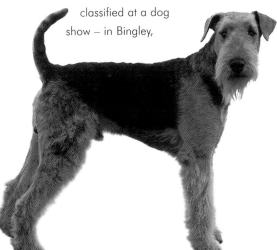

Other Names: Waterside terrier, Warfedale terrier, Bingley terrier
Date of Origin: 19th century
Place of Origin: Yorkshire, England
Original Use: Badger/otter hunting
Modern Use: Companion, guard dog, police dog (especially in Germany)
Size: Height: 22-24 in.
       Weight: 44-50 lb
Colors: All colors
Recognized by: A.K.C., K.C.

Yorkshire – under the auspices of the Airedale Agricultural Society and, from then on, in spite of its large size, the Airedale grew in popularity. Some dogs went to the U.S.A. where they excelled in the show ring, while others went to Germany, where they went to work pulling carts! Realizing their working abilities, the Germans began using them as guard dogs – they are born watchdogs and owners tell of how their behavior changes when dusk falls! – as border/frontier control dogs and as police dogs.

Undoubtedly their most attractive feature is their coat: a harsh, dense, wiry, coat usually rich tan and black, which requires regular trimming.

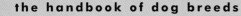

Australian Terrier

Other Names: **None**
Date of Origin: **19th century**
Place of Origin: **Australia**
Original Use: **Rat hunting, snake hunting**
Modern Use: **Farm 'pest controller', companion**
Size: Height: **10 in.**
    Weight: **12–14 lb**
Colors: **Blue-tan, sandy**
Recognized by: **A.K.C., K.C.**

Australia might be said to be the country that has specialized in producing unique animals: kangaroos, wallabies, and koala bears, as well as the world favourite pet bird, the budgerigar. The Australian terrier may be more orthodox, but it is no less significant – it is the only true terrier accepted by the world which did not originate in Britain.

Described as a 'canine cocktail' the Australian terriers were bred for work and, by the time they were shown in Australia in 1899, these tough and tenacious little dogs had been around for some 20 years. Most breeders today believe the terrier to be descended from numerous British terriers – especially the Yorkshire terrier on account of its size – as well as cairns, Irish, and Scottish terriers and possibly, Dandie Dinmonts, Skye, and Norwich terriers!

All these breeds travelled 'down under' with their owners and the welcome result was this low-set, compact, active, and agile dog that was able to kill a rat or rabbit in seconds. The Australian terrier, with its rugged appearance, made itself even more indispensable on remote farms where, as well as acting as an ever alert guard or watchdog, unlikely to back down from any confrontations with other dogs – or dingoes – or man, its keen eyesight and quick reflexes made them excellent snake hunters, killing by leaping off the ground, turning in mid-air to land behind the snake, which was then seized behind the neck.

While they are reasonably easy to train and make good companions, Australian terriers, like all terriers, have a strong independent streak.

Bedlington Terrier

This graceful, muscular British terrier, with its distinctive 'pear-shaped' head has existed for some 200 years and has a very different appearance from most other terriers: it's best described as a terrier in sheep's clothing. Not only does this rather accurately describe the Bedlington's outward appearance, but also its instincts as an effective hunter and killer.

Legend has it that the breed originated in the Rothbury Forest, on the Northumbrian borders of England and Scotland, where they were bred by gypsies for poaching, hunting badgers, and for racing. The Bedlington's distinctive hind legs and its speed do suggest that the whippet (see page 101) featured somewhere in its ancestry! The earliest recorded Bedlington – although not known by that breed name – is said to be a dog called Old Flint, owned by Squire Trevelyan in 1872, and whose descendants were said to be directly traceable until 1873. When the English Kennel Club was formed, more accurate records were kept, but the breed was then known as the Rothbury terrier, largely because one famous terrier called Piper Allan lived in that town. In 1825, Joseph Ainsley gave his dog Young Allan the breed name of Bedlington Terrier –

Other Names: Rothbury terrier
Date of Origin: 18th century
Place of Origin: Rothbury, on England/Scotland Borders, later Bedlington, Northumberland, England
Original Use: Rat/badger Hunting
Modern Use: Companion
Size: Height: 15–17 in.
   Weight: 17–23 lb
Colors: Liver, sandy, blue
Recognized by: A.K.C., K.C.

once again a Northumbrian name – and this became universally accepted.

At the beginning of the 20th century, this one time 'gypsy' poaching dog became a firm favourite in smart drawing rooms – where it cleverly displayed both good manners and a liking for the 'good life'!

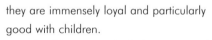

Border Terrier

Other Names: **None**
Date of Origin: **18th century**
Place of Origin: **Great Britain**
Original Use: **Ratting, harassing foxes from lairs**
Modern Use: **Hunt follower, companion**
Size: Height: **10–11 in.**
      Weight: **11–15 lb**
Colors: **Wheaten, tan-red, grizzle, blue-tan**
Recognized by: **A.K.C., K.C.**

In 1800, a Mr. James Davidson of Hyndlee wrote to a friend that he had bought 'twa (two) red devils o' terriers that has hard wiry coats and would worry any damned thing that crepit (moved)'. The 'red devils' he was describing were Border terriers.

Although the exact origins of the Border terrier are uncertain, it seems to have originated in the Cheviot Hills, the border between England and Scotland, where the breed has been known in its present form since the early 18th century. Small enough to follow a fox down a hole, but strong enough to enable it to keep up with horses at a hunt meet, the Border is quite possibly the terrier which has remained truest to its form and function – even though it may not now be used for its original uses of ratting and harassing foxes, as most Borders are destined to be companions and pets, for

they are immensely loyal and particularly good with children.

Its durable coat – which does not need to be stripped – protects it from the harshest northern weather, while its tail is a natural length – never docked – and is thick at the base, then tapering, set high and carried 'gaily'. Equally distinctive is the Border's head, which is required to resemble and otter and be moderately broad in the skull with a short, strong muzzle. The small, 'V'–shaped ears drop forwards to lie close to the dog's cheeks.

Cairn Terrier

One of Britain's most popular terriers, the cairn may have originated on the Scottish Isle of Skye. Scotland is the home of no fewer than five of the short-legged terrier breeds. The cairn terriers were a working breed which earned their living hunting vermin in the cairns – heaps of stones set up as landmarks and border markings – and searching for foxes. It was not until the early years of the 20th century, at dog shows, that the cairns became well known outside of the districts in which they lived and worked – the Western Highlands and Islands off the west coast of Scotland. Nevertheless, a cairn-type terrier can be seen in one of the most beautiful paintings, Jan Van Eyck's *Arnolfini Marriage* painted in 1434, and now in the National Gallery in London.

In some ways this anonymity meant that the cairn would not be 'prettied up' for the show ring, but would largely retain its sturdy body, natural shaggy coat, and its terrier instincts. The breed standard sums them up quite nicely: they are required to be fearless, gay, hardy, shaggy, and strong.

Stranding under 12 in. high and weighing an average of 14 lb, the cairn is happy to be picked up and carried under one arm – but much happier when running across a moor. They have a modest appetite for food – but a great lust for life, they like children and will even tolerate the family cat! All this and a terrier too! No wonder they are such a popular dog.

Other Names: **None**
Date of Origin: **Middle Ages**
Place of Origin: **Great Britain**
Original Use: **Ratting, fox hunting**
Modern Use: **Companion**
Size: Height: **10–12 in.**
    Weight: **13–16 lb**
Colors: **Cream, wheaten, red, grey, nearly black**
Recognized by: **A.K.C., K.C.**

Cesky Terrier

Other Names: **Czech terrier, Bohemian terrier**
Date of Origin: **1940s**
Place of Origin: **Czech Republic**
Original Use: **Burrowing and hunting**
Modern Use: **Hunting, companion**
Size: Height: **10–14 in.**
Weight: **12–18 lb**
Colors: **Blue-gray, tawny**
Recognized by: **K.C.**

This fearless and somewhat stubborn little dog was developed by a geneticist Dr. Frantisek Horak, from Klanovice, in former Czechoslovakia (now the Czech and the Slovak Republics) in the 1940s. Dr. Horak was interested in breeding a dog that worked like German hunting terriers – both above and below ground, in land or water, tracking and retrieving – but with shorter legs for more efficient tunnelling and working under ground. Tough, British terriers like the Sealyham, the Scottish and the Dandie Dinmont were used in the breeding process which resulted in the delightful cesky. It has all the 'ground' attributes of the typical terrier, combined with persistence and strength which enable it to subdue animals – and people – much larger than its

average 12 inches in height.

The cesky, like all terriers, is also a fine looking animal with a lovely blue-gray or fawn coat. The darker, wavy hair on the legs is not usually clipped, making for a lovely 'rippling' when the dog moves. The hair is not clipped on the head either, leaving prominent – and very distinguished looking – eyebrows and a beard over and around a well-developed nose, set off by triangular-shaped ears which fold forwards and lie close to the head. The tail is strong and tapers to a point and, when the dog is at rest, is carried down. Inquisitive and friendly – though like all terriers, apt to snap first and ask questions later – it's not surprising that the cesky is such a popular terrier, especially in its home countries of the Czech and the Slovak Republics.

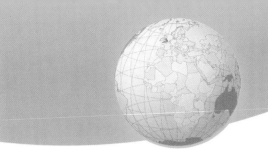

Dandie Dinmont Terrier

It is not certain whether the Dandie Dinmont is descended from the Skye, otterhound, Flanders basset hound, or even 'old-type' Scottish terriers, but we do know that the breed dates back to the 17th century. Paintings in many of the grand houses and castles of Scotland and the north of England show that it was owned by the aristocracy for centuries, although it was named after a character in Sir Walter

Other Names: **None**
Date of Origin: **17th century**
Place of Origin: **Great Britain**
Original Use: **badger/rat hunting**
Modern Use: **Companion**
Size: Height: **8–11 in.**
     Weight: **18–24 lb**
Colors: **Pepper, mustard**
Recognized by: **A.K.C., K.C.**

Scott's 19th-century novel *Guy Mannering*. 'Dandie Dinmont' was a Borders farmer who kept a pack of six terriers called Auld Pepper, Auld Mustard, Young Pepper, Young Mustard, Little Pepper and Little Mustard. Scott wrote that these dogs 'fear naething that ever cam wi' a hairy skin on't.'

One of the early owners of the 'type', if not the breed itself, was 'Piper' Allan of Northumberland – the same man credited with the development of the Bedlington terrier (see page 125). Allan's short-legged terriers caught the eye of the Duke of Northumberland, who evidently coveted a particular dog called Hitchem. When money was refused, the Duke offered Allan a farm in exchange for the dog – which was also refused. The Piper's son is said to have carried on the strain and one of the descendants of Hitchem was said to have been Auld Pepper.

Scott's novel did much to popularize 'all things Scottish', including the Dandie Dinmont terrier. Unlike other terriers, which are more 'square' in outline, Dandies are all flowing curves: a large round skull with a domed forehead, a gently arched back due to its long back legs and short front legs (which do make them prone to back pain and 'slipped discs') and a 'scimitar' like tail, about 8–10 in. long. Even the hair color is different: officially, Dandies are 'pepper' or 'mustard': more prosaically, the former is light gray to dark gray, and the latter, reddish brown to pale fawn. The Dandie's coat and beard texture are also unique, made up of a combination of hard and soft hairs.

Irish Terrier

Many enthusiasts of this handsome breed claim a long history and that it originated in the districts around Cork, Ireland and is descended from old black-and-tan and wheaten terriers. The first official mention of the Irish terrier, however, was not made until 1875 when a show in Dublin was organized for their debut. To most people's surprise, some 50 specimens of this formerly 'unknown' terrier were turned out for the event! The 'rules' — if that's what they could be called — were pretty 'loose', which no doubt was why, among the 50 entrants, dogs of various shapes, sizes and

Other Names: Irish red terrier, 'The dare devil'
Date of Origin: 18th century
Place of Origin: Ireland
Original Use: Vermin hunting, watchdog
Modern Use: Companion
Size: Height: 18–19 in.
     Weight: 25–27 lb
Colors: Always 'whole colored', either red, wheaten-red, yellow-red
Recognized by: A.K.C., K.C.

colors appeared: there was a class for dogs under 9 lb – no Irish terrier today weighs that little, so this was most likely a cairn Terrier in a bad disguise! Meanwhile, the winner of the Open Class weighed in at a hefty 30 lb, while one specimen was also said to be pure white in color! Although every dog was required to have a pedigree, the first-prize winner called Boxer, had a hand-written note attached to him stating 'bred by owner but pedigree unknown'!

Inevitably, arguments

followed – no doubt along with plenty of good stout! But, in 1879 a breed club was formed and the breed standard was issued which is little changed today. Irish terriers soon grew in popularity, not only because they excelled as gun dogs, were brilliant at ratting, rabbiting, fox hunting, and badger-facing (while their superb aquatic skills made them ideal otter hunters) but, because they were hardy, courageous, even-tempered, and trainable. Add to this their good looks and a delightful strutting walk – charming with a touch of Irish 'blarney' – the Irish terrier is, perhaps, one of the most elegant of all terriers. Yet a terrier it is: inquisitive, feisty, and, as its nickname suggests, a bit of a dare - devil, willing to take on any other dog it meets!

Jack Russell Terrier

When is a breed not a breed? When it's a Jack Russell! In fact the Kennel Club insists that this immensely popular terrier is not a breed but a 'type', because, to be recognized as a breed, there must be a breed standard which lays down the physical requirements. While every recognized breed has one – and there are around 400 recognized breeds – the Jack Russell doesn't. This is mostly because, while everyone can instantly identify them, they can't come to an agreement about exactly what they should look like! Arguments rage over leg length; whether ears should drop or be pricked up; coat colors and whether the coats should be smooth and soft, or wiry and shaggy.

One thing is certain, though, the Jack Russell terrier is not to be confused with the longer legged, officially recognized breed, the Parson Jack Russell terrier! This breed was developed for fox hunting: its longer legs enabled it to keep up with the horses. The Jack Russell terrier, which may be the result of accidental cross breeding with wire-haired fox terriers is also a hunter, but its speciality was rats – where there are horses there is corn and where there is corn, there are rats! The Jack Russell's continued existence is due to the fact that

Other Names: **None**
Date of Origin: **19th century**
Place of Origin: **Great Britain**
Original Use: **Ratting**
Modern Use: **Companion**
Size: Height: **10–12 in.**
　　　　Weight: **9–15 lb**
Colors: **White-brown, white-black, tricolor**
Recognized by: **Not recognized as a breed! Only recognized as a 'type'.**

these crossbred terriers were extremely valuable in controlling rodent populations – in the countryside and in towns: In the late 1970s, the Portuguese government employed a number of particularly enthusiastic Jack Russells from Yorkshire to help rid the capital city, Lisbon, of rats.

Like all terriers, Jack Russells can be snappy: when one goes for a wander, most people sensibly give them a wide berth – just in case! Nevertheless, they also have a great sense of humor, are devoted to their owners and are known to be among the best soccer players in the canine kingdom – although they're not too keen on passing the ball, generally defending it until it bursts, and tend to argue with the referee!

Kerry Blue Terrier

This handsome terrier from County Kerry, in the southwest of Ireland, is by government decree, the national dog of Ireland. Some legends maintain that the Kerry blue arrived in Ireland aboard Noah's Ark, while others tell of a dog shipwrecked off the coast, which swam ashore and proved to be such a fighter that he killed every dog he encountered and thus established the breed. The county never claimed the Kerry blue as its own, however: the link with the specific county in fact comes from Mrs. Casey Hewitt, from Tralee in County Kerry who first exhibited her dog at Cruft's in 1922. The same year, the Kennel Club officially recognized the breed.

Dogs of the Kerry blue 'type' are in fact indigenous to Ireland – there are also the Soft-coated wheaten (see page 145) and

Other Names: Irish blue terrier
Date of Origin: 18th century
Place of Origin: Co. Kerry, southwest Ireland
Original Use: Badger/fox/rat hunting
Modern Use: Field trials, rat/rabbit hunting, companion
Size: Height: 18–19 in.
　　　Weight: 33–37 lb
Colors: Any shade of blue
Recognized by: A.K.C., K.C.

Irish terriers (see page 131). The Irish peasant classes were forbidden to own hunting dogs like the Irish wolfhound (see page 97), but were permitted terriers because they hunted vermin. It seems likely that, either by chance or design, matings between the squires' Irish wolfhounds and the farmers' terriers did occur. Kerries were – and still are – excellent terriers, guard dogs, hard working farm dogs who will herd sheep and cattle, and who because they like water, will also retrieve water fowl, as well as excellent household companions.

The blue color of their coats, possibly originally a cloudy black, has been intensified by years of selective breeding.

135

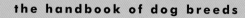

Lakeland Terrier

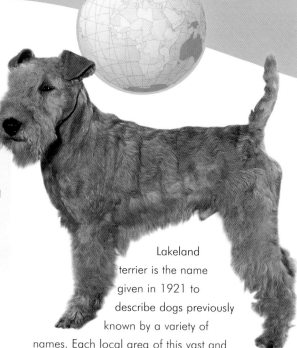

Other Names: **Variety of names depending on exact region, including Cumberland, Patterdale (see note below), fell terrier**

Date of Origin: **18th century**

Place of Origin: **Cumberland (Lake District), England**

Original Use: **Small mammal hunting (inc. foxes)**

Modern Use: **Companion**

Size: Height: **13–15 in.**

Weight: **15–17 lb**

Colors: **Black, blue, black-tan, blue-tan, red, wheaten**

Recognized by: **A.K.C., K.C.**

The Lakeland Terrier was bred in the Lake District, in the English county of Cumberland which borders onto Scotland. With lakes, mountains, and dales the region also had numerous foxes, which this agile terrier proved adept at pursuing and killing. Fox hunting in the region was not the 'well-dressed sport' of the more southern counties, and nor was it necessarily conducted on horseback, since most of the terrain was unsuitable for this type of pursuit. Instead, terriers were the order of the day because they would follow their quarry relentlessly over and under ground. The breed is likely to have descended from the now extinct black-and-tan terrier, which also gave rise to the Welsh terrier.

Lakeland terrier is the name given in 1921 to describe dogs previously known by a variety of names. Each local area of this vast and beautiful county bred 'killer terriers' with powerful jaws to see off the foxes that preyed on the sheep. Some of these terriers were called Cumberland terriers, others were fell terriers, and some were Patterdale terriers. This last terrier, which is also known as the black fell terrier continues to flourish, although it is not officially recognized as a breed by the Kennel Club.

In 1928 Lakeland terriers made their first appearance at a Kennel Club show: some doubted whether the terrier would ever be a success in the show ring, but they were very wrong. In 1967 Champion Stingray of Derryabah was judged Supreme Champion at Cruft's and the following year, was crowned Best In Show at Westminster.

Manchester Terrier

At the end of the 18th century, terriers were divided roughly by size (long or short legged), coat (smooth or wiry) and color (white, or black and tan). The Manchester was the long-legged, smooth-coated, black-and-tan terrier and then called simply the black-and-tan (although there was a wire-haired version which later became extinct, but left its tell-tale marks in other breeds such as the Airedale, (see page 123).

The Manchester terrier is one of the few smooth-coated terrier breeds. Said to have originated in the city of Manchester in England – although it was only named as such in the 1920s – it is thought to be the result of a mating between a much earlier breed known as the 'English terrier' and a whippet (see page 101). In general though, credit is given to Mr. John Hulme of Crumpsall, of Manchester, for developing the breed in the 19th century, which was as adept at catching rabbits in the field as it was at killing rats in a pit. When the 'sport' of ratting in pits was banned, the Manchester declined in numbers. This decline was further enhanced when the cropping of the dog's ears was outlawed: to protect the terriers ears from attack by vermin, the ears had always been cut short. Breeders received a shock when the saw the rather oversized ears of the Manchester for the first time in centuries! Breeders were soon able to produce ears that are as neat and attractive as any other terrier's, however.

Other Names: English gentleman's terrier, black-and-tan
Date of Origin: 16th century
Place of Origin: Manchester, Great Britain
Original Use: Ratting, rabbit hunting
Modern Use: Companion
Size: Height: 15–16 in.
Weight: 11–22 lb
Colors: Black with tan markings
Recognized by: A.K.C., K.C.

137

Norfolk Terrier

Other Names: Known in Britain until 1964, and still known in the U.S.A. as Norwich terriers
Date of Origin: 19th century
Place of Origin: East Anglia, Great Britain
Original Use: Ratting
Modern Use: Companion
Size: Height: 9½– 10 in.
Weight: 11–12 lb
Colors: Grizzle, black-tan, red, wheaten
Recognized by: A.K.C., K.C.

From around 1880 until 1965, the Norfolk terrier was known as the Norwich Terrier (see page 139). This is because the Norwich terrier produced puppies with both erect ears and with dropped ears. The two varieties existed side by side, were mated together, and competed against each other in the same class at shows. However, neither variety dominated and, far from merging together into one breed, the two varieties diverged in certain important characteristics, which inevitably led to arguments among breeders. In January 1965, the Kennel Club ruling was that the terriers with the pricked up ears would continue with their original name of Norwich terriers, after the city, while the drop eared terriers would be known as Norfolk terriers, after the county. (In the United States however, both varieties continue to be known as Norwich Terriers.)

So, while a new breed was officially 'born' in 1965, the fact was that the Norfolk terrier had already been around for nearly 100 years. The small, low dog makes a good companion today, yet it was bred for work – and is still very capable at doing it – displaying the true terrier-like desire to attack any rodent (and other small animal) that dares to show itself.

The coat is hard, straight and wiry, rarely are they 'barbered' or 'trimmed' in an overly elegant fashion, and most owners are happy for them to be 'natural' in appearance. This attitude has proved fortunate since it has preserved the weather proof qualities of the Norfolk terrier's coat.

Norwich Terrier

The Norwich terrier is among the smallest of the terriers and, with the Norfolk, is England's only short-legged terrier. The Norwich terrier has existed in the eastern counties of England for well over 100 years. Packs of small terriers, which had evolved from Irish terriers (see page 131) were in existence in the 19th century: in 1870 a gentleman known locally as 'Doggy Lawrence' made a good living for himself selling 'small red terriers' to the undergraduate students at Cambridge University, who kept the dogs as their mascots.

Others who acquired dogs from Doggy Lawrence included a Mr. Fred Law of Norfolk, who sent some to Mr. Jack Cooke, a well-known master of stag hounds, who in turn, employed one 'Rough-rider Jones'. When Jones left the master's employ, he took a few of the 'red terriers' with him – but rumor says he had already crossed these with Bedlington terriers

Other Names: Trumpington terrier, Jones terrier, Cantab terrier
Date of Origin: 19th century
Place of Origin: East Anglia, England
Original Use: Ratting
Modern Use: Companion
Size: Height: 10–10½ in.
      Weight: 11–12 lb
Colors: Grizzle, black-tan, red, wheaten
Recognized by: A.K.C., K.C.

and Staffordshire bull terriers. The red dogs at this time had no official name but were known locally as Trumpington terriers – although in parts of England and America, Rough-rider's legacy lived on in the name of Jones terrier, while their association with Cambridge University suggested to many the name of Cantab terriers.

Principally, these 'red terriers' were working dogs, ideally suited to ratting in the agricultural region of East Anglia, but their compact form also made them ideal pets. In 1932, they were granted official recognition as Norwich terriers, but were allowed to have either pricked up or dropped ears. Then, in 1965, came the split: the pricked-up-eared variety kept their name of Norwich terriers, while the drop-eared variety were now Norfolk terriers. In fact, the ear difference is often overplayed as the reason for the split: in truth, the two varieties of dog had developed along significantly different lines so that really, the ears had dogs of different shapes! The Norwich is a somewhat more 'low-slung' dog than the Norfolk!

Scottish Terrier

Other Names: **Aberdeen terrier, 'Scottie dog'**
Date of Origin: **19th century**
Place of Origin: **Scotland, Great Britain**
Original Use: **Badger, fox and vermin hunting**
Modern Use: **Companion**
Size: Height: **10–11 in.**
Weight: **19–23 kg**
Colors: **Black, black-brindle, red brindle, wheaten**
Recognized by: **A.K.C., K.C.**

One of the favorites among the terriers – and one of the 'heavyweights' among the small terriers – the 'Scottie' was previously known as the Aberdeen terrier. In the 18th century, the Highlands of Scotland were remote and quite inaccessible places, and the terriers varied from one district to the next, largely because most dogs resembled their parents who were local dogs and because breeders were keen on producing animals that were ideally suited to the land in which they worked. The Scottie's job was to destroy vermin: foxes, badgers, and other small mammals found in the rough countryside. Consequently a brave, tough dog, with an instinct for digging – preferably 'weatherproof' – was the order of the day.

When the Scottie was first shown at dog shows in the 19th century, it competed alongside the Dandie Dinmont and Skye terriers in 'Scotch terrier' classes, but in 1882, a breed club was formed and it was given a separate register, with the name Scottish Terrier. Although we tend to think that all Scotties are black in color – perhaps largely because of its starring role alongside the white West Highland terrier in advertising a famous whisky – the first standard of breed points said that the most desirable color was red-brindle with black muzzle and ear tips. Black Scotties were not even mentioned and don't seem to have been around until 1890, and it would be another 40 years or so before they became the most popular color.

Although the Scottie is no longer used for its original purpose, this fine terrier still retains all the attractive features of the breed: a little reserved and aloof – it leaves the 'excited nature' to the Westie! – as well as being independent and fiercely loyal to its owners.

Skye Terrier

Other Names: **None**
Date of Origin: **17th century**
Place of Origin: **Isle of Skye (in the Western Islands of Scotland)**
Original Use: **Small game hunting**
Modern Use: **Companion**
Size: Height: **9–10 in.**
       Weight: **19–23 lb**
Colors: **Black, gray, fawn, cream**
Recognized by: **A.K.C., K.C.**

This terrier, with its exceptionally long hair, hails from the Hebridean Island of Skye in Scotland where local legend claims that long-haired dogs swam ashore when ships of the Spanish Armada were wrecked by storms off the islands. (The same legend – but of surviving Spanish sailors – is also said to account for the magnificent patterns of Fair Isle jumpers!) The only flaw in the story is the fact that the long coat of the Skye terrier is, in fact, a recent 'invention'. The long coat was not apparent on one of the most famous terriers, Rona, owned by Queen Victoria.

In Scotland the dog's role was to catch and destroy vermin: foxes, badgers, even wild cats! This meant burrowing and digging and fighting in confined spaces – activities not to be hampered by an elaborate 'coiffure'.

Their powerful jaws are today hidden under magnificent whiskers: but it's still a brave – or foolhardy – person who tries to look! While Skyes are gentle and good-natured with their owners, they are very intolerant of strangers and will do more than snap! Skye owners are happy with the appearance and the character of these delightful terriers, and stand by the motto of the Skye Terrier Club of Scotland: "Wha dour meddle wi' me?" (Would you want to meddle with me?).

No reference to the Skye terrier could ever be complete without mentioning the world-famous Greyfriar's Bobby, one of the few dogs in Britain to have a memorial in Edinburgh, Scotland – and one that is a major tourist attraction as well.

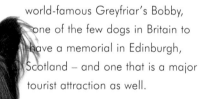

Smooth Fox Terrier

Other Names: **Fox terrier**
Date of Origin: **18th century**
Place of Origin: **Great Britain**
Original Use: **Fox flushing, vermin hunting**
Modern Use: **Companion**
Size: Height: **15–15½ in.**
Weight: **16–18 lb**
Colors: **Black-tan, white-tan, white**
Recognized by: **A.K.C., K.C.**

At one time, all dogs that 'went to earth' in the pursuit of foxes were called fox terriers, and every English county had its own version. It was not until 1850 that breeding was regularized, resulting in the breed today. The 'smooth' while never the most fashionable of terriers, has always been popular because of its hard-working 'no-nonsense' character, always ready to get on with the job. This breed began life in the stables, where it proved itself extremely adept at killing vermin, especially rats. And, if they had to dig them out first with their strong legs, then so much the better! Soon huntsmen began to exploit this tenacity to dig out foxes that had escaped down holes. This is probably how the terrier got its name – it's certainly more appealing than 'rat terrier', and the adjective 'smooth' exists to distinguish from its 'relative', the wire fox terrier.

In the early days of the breed, both varieties – smooth and wire – were bred together: a smooth called Jack is in fact the 'big daddy' of all the great wires as he was mated with a bitch of unknown ancestry – but obviously rough coated – called Trap.

The abundant coat of the smooth fox terrier is straight, flat, and hard in texture.

Three years after the English Kennel Club was established, in 1876, the smooths were given their separate register. While they have left their working past behind, fox terriers are still predominantly white in color, with black or tan patches, although smooths come also in black and tan colors: many of the huntsmen preferred largely white dogs since this readily distinguished the dogs from the quarry in the turmoil of the hunt.

Wire Fox Terrier

Other Names: Fox terrier
Date of Origin: 19th century
Place of Origin: Great Britain
Original Use: Fox flushing, vermin hunting
Modern Use: Companion
Size: Height: 15–15½ in.
      Weight: 16–18 lb
Colors: White-black, white-tan, white
Recognized by: A.K.C., K.C.

Like many other terriers, The wire fox terrier was 'Made in Britain' and designed to 'go to earth' after foxes. Shape was not so important as long as the dog was sturdy enough to gallop alongside horses. Ancestry was even less important since huntsmen who used terriers generally developed local varieties to suit the terrain in which they hunted, adding touches of 'outside' blood whenever they thought it advantageous. In the 18th century – and earlier – no one bothered to record the details, except to mention a particularly outstanding dog.

It seems likely that Old English rough terriers were used: in their own rights, these already were early types of dachshunds and beagles. Staffordshire bull terrier types were also likely to have been used which in time, would bring about the division in the two coats. From 1876, different registers were established for the different coated varieties, but crossbreeding between them was still allowed.

Around this time, the Fox Terrier Club was set up in England and it drew up the breed standard: straight legs, strong jaw, compact feet, a short back, well-curved stifles and sloping shoulders. It is said that the fox terrier was to be as close to being a horse as a dog could ever be! And, like a horse, fox terriers don't merely walk, they prance and dance – right on their tip toes! But some characteristics of the fox terrier are still truly terrier-like: these dogs just adore digging – almost as much as they like challenging other dogs to a fight!

Where the smooth fox terrier's coat is hard and flat, the wire fox terrier has a dense, wiry coat with a lovely dense set of facial whiskers. The wire fox terrier is permitted in white, white and tan, and white and black.

Soft-coated Wheaten Terrier

Although this terrier has a long history, it was not officially recognized until 1937 by the Irish Kennel Club and by the Kennel Club in England in 1943. A native of the Munster region in southwest Ireland, for centuries the soft-coated wheaten – whose name perfectly describes both its color and coat – was an 'all–purpose' working dog, used for driving cattle home, guarding and as an efficient 'pest controller'. Versatile dogs like these were developed to overcome the ancient laws in Ireland which prohibited peasants from owning hunting hounds. Terriers fitted the bill perfectly!

The soft-coated wheaten may have descended from the now extinct black-and-tan terrier and, although a slightly smaller and stockier dog, it is a relative of – and some hold, the ancestor of– the Kerry blue terrier (see page 135) and the Irish terrier (see page 131).

The breed is distinguished by its gorgeous, abundant , moderately long, soft and silky, and, slightly wavy coat that is the color – as the lyrical Irish say – 'of a field of ripening wheat in the morning sun'. Since its official

Other Names:	None
Date of Origin:	18th century
Place of Origin:	Munster, southwest Ireland
Original Use:	Herding, vermin hunting
Modern Use:	Companion
Size: Height:	18–19 in.
Weight:	35–45 lb
Colors:	Wheaten
Recognized by:	A.K.C., K.C.

recognition, this attractive and remarkably easy-going, even-tempered terrier has justifiably, become a firm favorite with owners on both sides of the Atlantic.

Staffordshire Bull Terrier

Other Names: **None**
Date of Origin: **19th century**
Place of Origin: **Great Britain**
Original Use: **Dog fighting, ratting**
Modern Use: **Companion**
Size: Height: **14–16 in.**
　　　Weight: **24–38 lb**
Colors: **Brindle, red, fawn, black, blue, white, or white with any of these colors**
Recognized by: **A.K.C., K.C.**

The well-muscled 'Staffie' did indeed originate in the Midlands county of Staffordshire, England. In the early 19th century, the two most popular 'sports' were bull baiting – in which dogs fought with bulls – and dog fighting, where a pair of dogs, matched in size and weight fought in a wooden sided pit. The dogs used to bait bulls were the earlier version of the modern bulldog (see page 180) with short legs, deep chests and short, massive jaws. The fighting dogs, on the other hand, could be of any shape whatsoever. What was needed was the strength and tenacity of the bulldog combined with the speed and agility of the terrier. It seems likely then that the Staffie is the result of crossing between bulldogs and Old English terriers.

In the 19th century, there was still a wide range of types in these fighting dogs – with each region claiming their dogs to be the 'perfect' combination. In 1835 bull baiting was outlawed in England; this led to an increased interest in dog fighting, using dogs variously described as 'pit dogs', 'pit bull terriers', and 'half and halfs'. When dog fighting was outlawed, many fights went 'underground' and continued well into the 20th century: some say it is because of these illegal fights that the breed survived. In 1935, however, the Staffie, shook off its fighting background and entered the show ring. A club was formed, a breed standard set and respectability earned in the form of official recognition in 1939 by the Kennel Club and a separate register for the breed.

Staffies are the terrier that many 'love to hate' for it has suffered from its former role as a fighter. Like all dogs of any breed, it thrives on affection, returning it tenfold, and is docile, unless encouraged to fight or attack.

West Highland White Terrier

The West Highland white terrier, or 'Westie' as it affectionately known throughout the world, shares the same mixed ancestry of the cairn terrier (see page 127). It has similar short legs, a foxy-faced head, harsh coat and rather gaily carried tail. The only difference is the color. White 'sports' have always appeared in dog breeds and, in the 17th century, King James I of England (VI of Scotland) is said to have sent to Argyllshire for 'six little white earth–dogges', which he gave as a present to the King of France.

By the end of the 19th century, most Cairn breeders disregarded the white pups but, thanks to the Malcolm family of Portalloch, the Westie was encouraged. The Malcolms rightly believed that a good terrier among the cairns was even better for being white – because it was easier to see! While most cairn breeders were desperately trying to rid themselves of white dogs, the

Other Names: 'The Westie'
Date of Origin: 19th century
Place of Origin: Scotland
Original Use: Ratting
Modern Use: Companion
Size: Height: 10–11 in.
Weight: 15–22 lb
Colors: White
Recognized by: A.K.C., K.C.

Malcolms worked to remove colored dogs from their strain! In 1900, Colonel Malcolm introduced the West Highland white terrier into the show ring and, in 1907, the Kennel Club recognized it as a breed – two years before the cairn itself was officially recognized!

A great favorite at dog shows, the Westie is also famous worldwide for its part in advertising a particular Scotch Whisky. It is also a great favorite in the home: it has all the courage of a terrier, but will seldom pick a fight; it enjoys the outdoor life but is equally happy and content on the sofas of suburbia. It likes modest amounts of exercise followed by a snooze, and it's a very smart–looking dog that doesn't need a great deal of 'primping': although it is white, the harsh coat sheds dirt as easily as it sheds water – but mostly over those sofas!

Toy Dogs

Toy dogs were generally bred as pets and companions, although many, like the affenpinscher (see page 151) also did very useful jobs as 'pest controllers' and acted as fearless guard dogs in spite of their size. Toy dogs are not a recent development: some toy breeds have been around for at least 2,000 years in both Europe, where they were also known as 'lap dogs', and in the Far East, where some were called 'sleeve dogs' because their size enabled them to be carried in the silk sleeves of kimonos and similarly styled robes.

AFFENPINSCHER

PEKINGESE

Most toy breeds are related to larger breeds in other groups and, in spite of their size, they maintain all of the characteristics of their larger relatives. 'Toys' only in name, they are most definitely dogs, and some toys can be as formidable as their 'big brothers'!

149

MALTESE

The most ancient of the toy breeds is thought to be the 'lion dog of Peking' better known toady as the Pekingese (see page 171) which was bred to reflect the leonine spirit of the Buddha. This little dog later became a favorite at the Imperial Chinese court and was often given as a diplomatic gift to visiting dignitaries from other countries. The cult of the lap dog in China reached its peak between 1820 and 1850 under the reign of the Dowager Empress Tzu Hsi, whose 4,000 eunuchs housed in the 'forty-eight palaces' were employed solely to breed Pekingese.

In the West, the Romans are credited with developing the oldest European toy breed, the little white Maltese (see page 155). Throughout European history, toy dogs were a symbol of luxury and wealth to be enjoyed – and pampered – by the rich and leisured classes. Many toy dogs became firm favorites at the royal and noble courts and appear in some of the most famous paintings of Western art: Veronese, Rubens and Rembrandt painted papillons (see page 170), as did the American-born artist, Benjamin West. Many of Thomas Gainsborough's elegant subjects for his portraits chose to be accompanied by their Pomeranians (see page 172).

POMERANIAN

PAPILLON

Affenpinscher

In German, *affen* means 'to mock' or 'tease', and *affenartig* means 'monkey-like'. The delightful little affenpinscher, is sometimes called the 'monkey terrier' and people who see the dog for the first time invariably comment on its resemblance to this animal. Despite this comical appearance the affenpinscher's tightly compressed jaws still make it a formidable mouser and ratter given the chance.

The origins of the breed are obscure but thought, perhaps, to be from crosses between pug-like dogs from Asia and small German pinschers. The affenpinscher is also thought to be the likely progenitor of the griffon Bruxellois (Brussels griffon) and a relative of the miniature schnauzer.

Today, in Germany, the breed is quite rare, but is thriving in North America where, despite the fact that it is an incredibly stubborn little dog – so is quite hard to obedience-train – and, like all terriers, has a tendency to snap, it has found itself a happy niche as a lively companion dog.

Other Names: **Monkey dog**
Date of Origin: **17th century**
Place of Origin: **Germany**
Original Use: **Vermin hunting, companion**
Modern Use: **Companion**
Size: Height: **10–12 in.**
      Weight: **7–8 lb**
Colors: **Black**
Recognized by: **A.K.C., K.C.**

Australian Silky Terrier

Other Names: **Silky, silky terrier, Sydney silky**
Date of Origin: **20th century**
Place of Origin: **Australia**
Original Use: **Companion**
Modern Use: **Companion**
Size: Height: **9 in.**
    Weight: **8–11 lb**
Colors: **Blue-tan**
Recognized by: **A.K.C., K.C.**

Originally called the 'Sydney silky', since it was in Sydney, New South Wales, that the breed was first developed in the early 20th century, the silky is basically a cross between the Australian terrier (see page 124) and the Yorkshire terrier (see page 176) – with perhaps just a touch of Norwich terrier (see page 139) in there for good measure. The gorgeous silky coat – which is fine, and has a mirror-like gloss to it – comes from the influence of a hidden ancestor, the early Skye terrier (see page 142) that was used to develop the Australian terrier. The color is called 'blue' by breeders and may be 'silver-blue', 'pigeon-blue' or 'slate-blue' with rich tan-colored hairs growing down from the knees to the feet. The breed was developed by fanciers who felt there was a need for a small terrier which would be suited to 'modern' Australian life in city apartments.

First shown in Australia in 1907, when the breed standard allowed ears to be either pricked or folded (today they are pricked), the silky reached England in 1928. Despite its obvious good looks, the silky did not gain widespread recognition until the 1940s.

American military and civilian personnel, who arrived in Australia during World War II, took it to their hearts – and back to their homes overseas, where the little dog is now established as a firm favorite.

Bichon Frise

Other Names: **Tenerife dog**
Date of Origin: **Middle Ages**
Place of Origin: **Southern Mediterranean regions**
Original Use: **Companion**
Modern Use: **Companion**
Size: Height: **9–11 in.**
        Weight: **7–12 lb**
Colors: **White**
Recognized by: **A.K.C., K.C.**

The term 'bichon' is often used to refer to a family of small, usually white, dogs, to which the bichon frise and the Maltese (see page 155) belong, and which originated in the Mediterranean region around 500 BC. 'Bichon' in French means 'lap dog', and these animals have always been bred as companions and pets.

'Frise' (or curled) refers to the coat of soft corkscrew curls which, with careful trimming for the show ring, makes the delightful little dog look as fluffed-up as a pyjama case! Attractive, happy, lively – in short, downright cute – the bichon frise is also a real 'goer': Norwegian farmers have found that this toy breed is very adept at rounding up sheep! Perhaps the sheep mistake them for very clever lambs!

By the 14th century, Spanish sailors introduced the bichon frise to Tenerife in the Canary Islands, where it was rediscovered by Italian sailors who took them home, where they became favorites in the palaces of nobles before spreading across Europe. Although it

has an ancient lineage, the bichon frise is a relative newcomer to the official canine world: it was only officially recognized in both Britain and the United States in the 1970s. Nevertheless, the bichon frise has a firm, loyal and growing following of admirers.

Bolognese

Other Names: Bichon Bolognese
Date of Origin: Middle Ages
Place of Origin: Italy
Original Use: Companion
Modern Use: Companion
Size: Height: 10–12 in.
Weight: 5–9 lb
Colors: White
Recognized by: K.C.

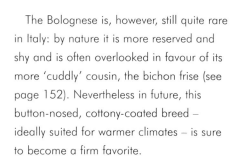

Although this white dog takes its name from the northern Italian city of Bologna, it seems likely that the Bolognese is descended from the bichons that originated in the more southern Mediterranean regions. The Bolognese, like all the bichons, has a very long history and numerous descriptions of the breed have been recorded since the 12th century. Like other toy dogs, the Bolognese was a companion dog and highly desired at the courts of Renaissance princes including the Medici in Florence, the d'Este family in Ferrara, and the Gonzagas in Mantua. A very similar looking dog to the Bolognese appears in a fresco painted between 1465–74, in the Palazzo Ducale in Mantua, by Andrea Mantegna.

The Bolognese is, however, still quite rare in Italy: by nature it is more reserved and shy and is often overlooked in favour of its more 'cuddly' cousin, the bichon frise (see page 152). Nevertheless in future, this button-nosed, cottony-coated breed – ideally suited for warmer climates – is sure to become a firm favorite.

Maltese

Other Names: **Bichon Maltais**
Date of Origin: **Antiquity**
Place of Origin: **Mediterranean region**
Original Use: **Companion**
Modern Use: **Companion**
Size: Height: **8–10 in.**
Weight: **4–6 lb**
Colors: **White**
Recognized by: **A.K.C., K.C.**

These pure white, long, silky-haired, good-natured and happy little dogs were once called Maltese terriers – but neither in design nor temperament is the Maltese a terrier. Arguments rage around the origins of the Maltese's name: Dr. Caius wrote that they were called 'Meliti', meaning 'of the island of Malta' and described them as very small and popular with ladies who would carry them in their 'arms, their bosoms and their beds'! But 1,500 years earlier, Strabo, wrote in AD 25 that there was a town in Sicily called Melita which exported beautiful dogs called 'Canis Melitei'. When Strabo was writing, a Maltese was known to be on Malta: it was called Issa and belonged to Pubilus, the Roman governor of the island, who is reputed to have been so entranced by her looks that he had her portrait painted.

I like to think though, that whichever Meliti or *Melitei* the Maltese came from, both names are derived from the Latin word *melli* which means 'honey' and perfectly describes the sweet nature of the breed! However, archaeological evidence suggests that in fact the Maltese has an even longer history than even Strabo suggested, for images of similar looking dogs are to be found in ancient Egyptian tombs.

It seems the good fortune of the Maltese to have been captured on canvas: Sir Joshua Reynold's 1763 portrait of Nellie O'Brien includes an unmistakable Maltese, while later, Sir Edward Landseer, incorrectly prophesied the breed's demise in his 1840 painting *The Last of the Race*. With so many admirers across the world, the Maltese is certain to remain one of the most popular toy breeds.

Havanese

Other Names: **Bichon Havanais, Havana silk dog**
Date of Origin: **18–19th centuries**
Place of Origin: **Mediterranean regions/Cuba**
Original Use: **Companion**
Modern Use: **Companion**
Size: Height: **8–11 in.**
      Weight: **7–13 lb**
Colors: **Silver, cream, gold, blue, black**
Recognized by: **A.K.C., K.C.**

The shy, gentle Havanese, which becomes a devoted companion to its human 'family' may be descended from Bolognese (see page 154) crosses with small poodles (see page 194): many Bolognese found their way to Argentina as the pets of wealthy Italians in the 18th and 19th centuries before arriving in Cuba, while Spanish-owned Maltese were already likely to be present on the island. In postrevolutionary Cuba the little Havanese did not fare very well: in the aftermath of most political revolutions, the political and cultural signs and symbols of the former system of rule are obliterated — either deliberately or through neglect. Consequently, the Havanese is rare in Cuba, but is immensely popular in the United States — especially among Cuban expatriates. Although similar to the other 'bichon' breeds, unlike them, the Havanese appears in a range of gorgeous colors: cream, silver, gold, blue and black — but not white! With its large dark eyes, and lovely feathery-haired coat and tail of long, silky hair, coupled with a delightful character, the Havanese is set to win plenty of hearts!

Chihuahua

The origins of the Chihuahua, named after the Mexican state from which it was first exported, are shrouded in myth and legend. What is fact is that the little Chihuahua is the world's smallest breed of dog – a mere 2–4 lb is the average weight. It is also remarkable as the Chihuahua sometimes has a hole in its head: this is the mollera or fontanelle, an area of membranous space between the cranial bones that exists in foetal life and in infancy – even in human babies – but which, in some Chihuahuas, fails to close. Not all Chihuahuas have a mollera, but the condition is largely restricted to the breed.

Some claim the Chihuahua was a breed developed by the Aztecs from dogs brought to the New World by the Spanish Conquistadors. Others, that the ancestor of the Chihuahua was already in the region when the Spanish arrived: the Aztec name Xoloitzcuintli is often taken to refer to the Chihuahua but, in truth this was a much larger animal, possibly a coatimundi. There are also further unsubstantiated legends that Chihuahuas with red coats were

Other Names: None
Date of Origin: disputed: 16th century or 19th century
Place of Origin: Mexico
Original Use: Companion
Modern Use: Companion
Size: Height: 6–9 in.
Weight: 2–6 lb
Colors: Any
Recognized by: A.K.C., K.C.

ritually sacrificed on funeral pyres. However, since the Aztec civilization was destroyed by the European invasion, it may be that the dog was in fact 'rescued' by the Spanish who then developed the breed. There is no mention of such a small dog between the time of Cortes's conquest in 1519 and the late 19th century: the Pelon or Mexican hairless dog was known to be inhabiting the border towns of Mexico and America in the 1840s and, in the 1850s, the Chihuahua was being exported to the U.S.A.. The first Chihuahua to be registered in the U.S.A. was the appropriately named Midget in 1904. Many breeders believed that the long-coat Chihuahua was the 'original', but it was the short-coated variety that caught the attention of the public.

Whatever the origins of the Chihuahua, there is no doubting the immense popularity of the breed, which is happiest when it is in the lap of its owner! These may be tiny dogs, but they possess giant personalities: fearless and very agile, they could easily be called 'Mexican spitfires'.

Chinese Crested Dog

The Chinese crested is one of a small group of hairless breeds – although a luxuriously coated powderpuff variety does also exist. Hairless dogs have appeared in many parts of the world and, in general, they have been named after their place of origin, such as the African sand dog, the Mexican hairless, and the Abyssinian hairless dog. There is, however, no documented proof that the Chinese crested originated in China, since evidence suggests that hairless dogs originated in Africa before they were transported to Asia and America. The reason for hairlessness has been attributed to an incompletely functioning gene, to a blood factor deficiency and to a skin ailment involving

Other Names: Powderpuff, Turkish hairless, Chinese hairless
Date of Origin: Antiquity
Place of Origin: China/Africa
Original Use: Companion
Modern Use: Companion
Size: Height: 9–13 in.
       Weight: 5–12 lb
Colors: Variety
Recognized by: A.K.C., K.C.

pigmentation. Whatever the cause, hairlessness is sex-linked to missing or abnormal teeth and toenails, so hairless dogs do not breed very successfully. However, matings between two hairless dogs can also result in 'coated' puppies, called powderpuffs. These powderpuffs are genetically more 'sound' and are the key to safeguarding the future of this interesting and delicate breed of dogs.

The skin of the Chinese crested is soft and smooth – and can be any color, including spotted and dappled with bronze, blue or gray. The colors do vary in summer and winter: a careful watch needs to be kept so that they don't get sunburnt or chilled. Because of the lack of hair, the Chinese crested is odorless, and it won't leave hair all over your chairs! The only hair is the very fine, silky crest on the top of the skull, feathering on the feet and a plume on the end of the tail. The ears, which are large and erect may also be 'fringed' with hair. The powderpuffs have a coat of very fine hair which can be either long or short: among breeders the coat is called poetically, a 'veil coat'. At first sight, it is easy to be shocked or put off by a hairless dog but, after a few minutes, the expressive face, the liveliness and affectionate character of these little dogs invariably wins over many hearts.

English Toy Terrier

Other Names: **Black-and-tan toy terrier, toy Manchester terrier**
Date of Origin: **19th century**
Place of Origin: **Great Britain**
Original Use: **Ratting, rabbit hunting**
Modern Use: **Companion**
Size: Height: **10–12 in.**
Weight: **6–8 lb**
Colors: **Black-tan**
Recognized by: **A.K.C., K.C.**

These terriers are relatively rare – even in Britain where they originated. They descended from runt Manchester terriers (see page 137) and were called toy Manchesters, before being called toy black-and-tan terriers and then miniature black-and-tan terriers before they adopted their present name in 1962 (although in the United States they are still called toy Manchesters!). Small, yet spirited, these are terriers through and through.

The first known mention of them occurs in Dr. Caius' *Of Englishe Dogges* from 1570, although he did not make any distinction between the 'normal–sized' Manchester terrier and the bantam version and it seems that small offspring were often the product of normal–sized parents.

In the mid-19th century, the mini-dogs were quite common, and were especially favoured in the 'sporting' rat pits in the north of England. Around the same time there were rumors of crosses to other breeds, in particular the dachshund (see page 109) and the whippet (see page 101) as well as Italian greyhounds (see page 163) which would have stabilized the English toy terriers' size and would account for the slightly arched or, 'roached' back. At various stages in its development, breeders have emphasized different characteristics: at one time, the small size was all important, at other times, it was the 'candle-flame' ears.

One thing that was insisted on at all times was the precise black-and-tan markings.

Griffon Bruxellois

Other Names: **Brussels griffon, griffon Belge**
Date of Origin: **19th century**
Place of Origin: **Belgium**
Original Use: **Vermin hunting**
Modern Use: **Companion**
Size: Height: **7–8 in.**
      Weight: **6–12 lb**
Colors: **Black, black-tan**
Recognized by: **A.K.C., K.C.**

It would be nice to think of the delightful griffon bruxellois as the perfect symbol of European unity and accord: here is a breed that is the result of blending bloodlines from diverse regions to produce a friendly, alert, attractive companion. Their mixed ancestry is thought to include among others, the griffon d'ecurie (stable griffon) which was crossed with the English toy spaniel in the 19th century, plus additions from the German affenpinscher (see page 151), the miniature black-and-tan terriers, Yorkshire terriers (see page 176), the Dutch smoushond, the French barbet, and pugs (see page 175). But dissent remains – in the naming of the breed! In some countries (especially Belgium) three dogs are classified as Belgian griffons while, in other countries, each dog is recognized as a unique breed.

Originally, the griffon bruxellois was used as a pest controller in the stables of Brussels – especially those which housed the horses that pulled *fiacres* (hansom cabs). It seems that these dogs were so determined to be with their owners – or possibly the horses – at all times, that they took to sitting on the front seats of the cabs when they were driven around the city and became the self-appointed guardians of the transport system! Today, many cab drivers in Brussels have a picture sticker of a griffon bruxellois attached to their windshields in honor of this canine companion!

Griffon means 'wiry' and refers to the rough coat of the breed, although smooth-coated 'petit brabacon' puppies can be born to wiry parents.

Italian Greyhound

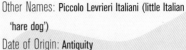

Other Names: Piccolo Levrieri Italiani (little Italian 'hare dog')
Date of Origin: Antiquity
Place of Origin: Italy
Original Use: Companion
Modern Use: Companion
Size: Height: 13–15 in.
      Weight: 7–8 lb
Colors: Black, blue, fawn, cream
Recognized by: A.K.C., K.C.

The diminutive Italian greyhound belongs to the same family of sight hounds as the Irish wolfhound – the largest breed in the world (see page 97). The high-stepping little Italian is a perfect miniature of 'big' greyhounds, and the breed dates back to ancient Greek and Egyptian times, since there are numerous representations of them in ancient artworks as companions to pharaohs and heroes. Elegant and graceful, and a dog purely for pleasure rather than utility, it is not surprising that the Italian greyhound found favor with the rich and noble families of Europe from the Renaissance onwards: Frederick II the Great, King of Prussia (1712–1786), owned more than 50 of the little dogs and took great interest in employing only 'suitable people' to care for them. Charles

163

I of England (1600–1649), known for his love of dogs – and condemned by his critics for it – was familiar with the breed: his mother, Anne of Denmark was painted with five of the companion dogs. More surprising is the story that the 19th century Matabele chief, King Lobengula, was so fascinated with the high-stepping gait of the Italian greyhound that he 'paid' 200 head of cattle one! Owners and admirers of the breed would argue that this was a very small price to pay for such an ideal companion.

With their slim, highly refined body and delicate pencil-slim legs, the Italian greyhound does need a little extra special care: they injure easily – largely because they 'forget' their size and enjoy bursts of activity – and they are more susceptible to cold and wet. But, perhaps because they are Italians, they are able wear those special little 'doggy jackets' with such style!

Japanese Chin

Other Names: **Japanese spaniel, Chin**
Date of Origin: **Middle Ages**
Place of Origin: **Japan**
Original Use: **Companion**
Modern Use: **Companion**
Size: Height: **9–10 in.**
        Weight: **4–11 lb**
Colors: **Black-white, red-white**
Recognized by: **A.K.C., K.C.**

Dainty is word often used to describe the Chin – also known as the Japanese spaniel. While it is similar to the Pekingese (see page 171) the Chin is more likely to have evolved from the Tibetan spaniel (see page 199), which may have been introduced to Japan by Buddhist monks as early as 520 AD. They then became favorites in the royal households as highly prized, and very valuable, companion pets: even when Portuguese traders arrived in the 16th century, few Chin left Japan save for some presented to Princess Catherine of Braganza. The American naval commander, Commodore Perry took some Chins home on his return voyage in 1853. Only two survived the long sea journey to New York where they were presented to August Belmont. These two are reputed to

have died without issue but it was the start of great interest in the breed in the west and led to a great number of importations – and a fair number of myths. One legend says that the Chin was dwarfed through sake, Japanese rice wine!

The Chin arrived in Britain in 1880 where it was crossed with 'native' toy spaniels – which accounts today for the close similarity between the Chin and the King Charles Spaniel (see page 166). Like all breeds with flat faces, the Chin can suffer from respiratory and related cardiac problems. Still popular in Japan, the Chin was largely eclipsed in the West with the arrival of the Pekingese, but since the 1960s, there has been a resurgence of interest in these stylish little dogs with their large dark eyes and long straight coats.

King Charles Spaniel

Other Names: **English toy spaniel, 'Charlie'**
Date of Origin: **17th century**
Place of Origin: **Great Britain**
Original Use: **Companion**
Modern Use: **Companion**
Size: Height: **10–11 in.**
     Weight: **8–14 lb**
Colors: **Tricolor, black-tan, red-tan, Blenhiem (pearly white with chestnut-red patches)**
Recognized by: **K.C.**

The King Charles Spaniel is a compact little dog with a larger head and less tapered muzzle than its close relative the Cavalier King Charles. Small spaniels were well known in Britain (and Europe) from the Middle Ages onwards, as spaniels of various sizes often occurred in single litters. Selective breeding in the 16th century of the smallest individuals led to the 'toy spaniel': Mary, Queen of Scots had a pack and, at the time of her execution, one devoted dog is said to have crept under her skirts and fought with the executioner who tried to remove it.

It was her great-grandson, King Charles II, who was to give his name to the breed, and who was one of its most devoted fans. The diarist of the Great Plague and the Fire

of London, Samuel Pepys noted that the spaniels had access to all parts of the palace of Whitehall, even on state occasions. The king would also be condemned for spending more time with his dogs than with affairs of state. King Charles's dogs were slightly larger and had longer noses than today's breed: interbreeding with Pekingese (see page 171), pugs (see page 175) and in particular, Japanese Chin (see page 165) were responsible for achieving the modern form. A trace of the Japanese Chin ancestry can be seen in the white blaze on the King Charles' forehead: this mark is said to be the thumb mark of the Buddha, left behind on the Chin when he blessed the dog.

Löwchen

Other Names: Petit chien lion (little lion dog)
Date of Origin: 17th century
Place of Origin: France
Original Use: Companion
Modern Use: Companion
Size: Height: 10–13 in.
      Weight: 9–18 lb
Colors: Any
Recognized by: A.K.C., K.C.

Many dogs have been called 'lion dogs' because of their appearance, but few look more leonine than the little löwchen, particularly when its coat has been clipped in the rather fancy manner! An ancient breed, the löwchen is possibly related to the small 'barbets' or water spaniel and to the bichon dogs from the Mediterranean regions. It can also be seen in a number of paintings by the masters of European art including Lucas Cranach the Elder and Francisco Goya.

Although the modern löwchen can be up to 13 in. high, it has been classed with the toy dogs since it was first registered in 1971. It is a strongly built dog with well-muscled hind quarters. These are left 'nude' for the show ring: the coat on the hind quarters is clipped out like a poodle (see page194), but left on the forequarters to form a mane. Tufts of hair are left on the end of the tail – which is carried over the back when the dog is on the move – and there are bracelets of hair around the 'wrists' and ankle joints. The clipped area is often a different shade and makes a tonal contrast with the longer coat.

Miniature Pinscher

Other Names: **Zwergpinscher, reh pinscher 'min pin'**
Date of Origin: **18th century**
Place of Origin: **Germany**
Original Use: **Ratting**
Modern Use: **Companion**
Size: Height: **10–12 in.**
Weight: **8–10 lb**
Colors: **Nearly black, chocolate, blue, red**
Recognized by: **A.K.C., K.C.**

The miniature pinscher belongs to the pinscher-schnauzer group of breeds which were developed in Germany. By no means a modern breed, small pinschers have been around since at least the 16th century, although unlikely to have been as small as today's 'min pin'. Nevertheless, the min pin shares its ancestors' love of hunting and chasing, and was kept in German farms and warehouses as an effective pest controller. Although today's min pin is strikingly similar to the English toy terrier, the two breeds evolved along different lines. The min pin also looks like a 'miniature Doberman': in fact the min pin predates the Doberman by some 200 years.

It has been suggested that, in the 19th century, to improve the quality and reduce the size of the miniature pinscher, dachshunds (see page 109) and Italian greyhounds (see page 163) were used in breeding programs. The clear red coloring could well have come from the dachshund, and may have led the min pin to be called 'reh pinscher' after the roe deer which were abundant in Germany at this time. Black, blue, and chocolate dogs with clearly defined rich tan markings are also recognized in the show rings. From the Italian greyhound the min pin could have obtained its distinctive high-stepping gait: each foot is lifted high like a little Hackney horse. A true terrier, the miniature pinscher's 'ratting abilities' remain undiminished and, like many terriers, it will challenge anyone – and any dog – snapping first and asking questions later.

Papillon

Other Names: **Continental toy spaniel**
Date of Origin: **17th century**
Place of Origin: **Continental Europe**
Original Use: **Companion**
Modern Use: **Companion**
Size: Height: **8–11 in.**
  Weight: **9–10 lb**
Colors: **White with patches of any color except liver**
Recognized by: **A.K.C., K.C.**

'Papillon' is French for 'butterfly' and is the name given to this little spitz-type dog for an obvious reason: their heads have a thin white blaze running down the eyes and are framed on either side by pricked flared and fringed ears which makes them resemble butterflies. Drop ears are also permissible, however, but these dogs are correctly called *phalene* – which means 'moth' (in North America they are known as Epagneul Nain). The delightful papillon is probably the most painted dog in the history of European art: they appear in paintings by Rubens, Van Dyck, Rembrandt and Fragonard, and famous owners in the past have included Madame de Pompadour and Queen Marie Antoinette.

The origins of the papillon are unknown and, to add confusion, some maintain they are descended from the 16th-century Spanish dwarf spaniel. Whatever its origins, the papillon was very well known across continental Europe by this time. It was perhaps because of their small size that they were able to be transported so easily! It also seems that some travelled with their Spanish and Italian owners to Central and South America.

The gorgeous coat is moderately long, fine and very silky. It falls flat on the body but forms a lovely ruff on the chest. The tail, likewise, is magnificently plumed and carried proudly over the back when this little dog moves at speed the 'feathers' stream out behind like a banner!

Pekingese

Now among the favorite toy dogs in the West, the Pekingese is almost extinct in its native China following the edicts of the Cultural Revolution, which banned all dogs from mainland China. The Chinese bred miniature dogs some 1,500 years ago: in AD 565 the emperor gave the name *ch'ih hu* or 'red tiger' to one such dog which rode with the emperor on his horse. Pekes were, at one time, bred exclusively at the royal courts of the Chinese emperors and the cult of the lap dog really reached its peak in the 19th century under the Dowager Empress, Tzu Hsi.

The Empress encouraged the development of 'lion dogs' linking them – and herself – to the spirit lions of the Buddha, and maintained 4,000 eunuchs whose task it was to produce these dogs. One of her acts was to compose a set of rules regarding their appearance: they were to have a 'swelling cape of dignity' round their necks, bent legs so they couldn't wander far from the palace – and her presence – and a coat the color of a lion. She also recommended a diet of sharks' fins, curlews' livers, and the breasts of quails. Such a pampered upbringing may account for the distinctly 'snobbish' character of the Peke and its stubborn

Other Names: **Peking palasthund, Peke**
Date of Origin: **Antiquity**
Place of Origin: **China**
Original Use: **Companion**
Modern Use: **Companion**
Size: Height: **6–9 in.**
　　　Weight: **7–12 lb**
Colors: **Any colors**
Recognized by: **A.K.C., K.C.**

streak. It is so superior that it will steadfastly refuse to do anything – even move – if it doesn't want to! More poetically, Chinese legend claims that the Peke is the result of a union between a lion and a monkey: it certainly has the nobleness of the former, while the monkey perhaps is responsible for its wilful streak!

Legend tells of how the Peke came to the West: on the sacking of Peking in 1860, four Pekes were 'captured' and one was presented to Queen Victoria.

Pomeranian

Other Names: Dwarf spitz, loulou
Date of Origin: Middle Ages, developed in the 19th century
Place of Origin: Germany
Original Use: Companion
Modern Use: Companion
Size: Height: 8½–11 in.
Weight: (4–5½ lb)
Colors: Black, brown, gray, blue, red, orange, cream, white, sable
Recognized by: A.K.C., K.C.

The classic spitz shape, 'fluffy' coat, and curled tail, illustrate the early origins of the Pomeranian in the larger spitz dogs of the Arctic Circle. In the Middle Ages, when the breed was first noted, it was found only in northern Germany – in Pomerania – from where it took its name. These early dogs were larger – and whiter – than the modern version: some were used as herding dogs and some were so large they were used as draft animals. When they first arrived in England in the 19th century, the Pomeranian did not excite any particular interest – England had its own herding breeds and didn't use dogs as draft animals and, since it had no sporting use, it came to be ignored.

That was until Queen Victoria visited Florence, Italy, in 1888, saw some Pomeranians and accepted one as a gift. Soon after she founded a kennel of the breed and began to exhibit them regularly, favoring the smaller-sized dogs between 12–16 lb. Following her royal example, other breeders began bantamizing and produced dogs of a mere 6 lb in weight – so even the Queen's smallest 'Poms' started to look enormous! Breeders were also able

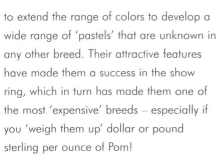

to extend the range of colors to develop a wide range of 'pastels' that are unknown in any other breed. Their attractive features have made them a success in the show ring, which in turn has made them one of the most 'expensive' breeds — especially if you 'weigh them up' dollar or pound sterling per ounce of Pom!

Despite its miniaturisation, like all toy breeds, the Pom still thinks and acts like a big dog. A fine bark makes it a terrific watchdog and the heart of a lion makes it a fearless — and devoted — companion.

173

Toy Poodle

Other Names: **Caniche, barbone**
Date of Origin: **16th century**
Place of Origin: **France**
Original Use: **Companion**
Modern Use: **Companion**
Size: Height: **11–15 in.**
Weight: **14–16 lb**
Colors: **All solid colors**
Recognized by: **A.K.C., K.C.**

In Britain, the toy poodle is classified alongside its 'bigger brothers', the standard and miniature poodles in the utility dog category, while in the U.S.A., it appears in the toy dogs category.

The original standard-sized dog was bred in Germany in the Middle Ages, as a 'water retriever', and was most likely taken from Germany to France in the 16th century, where it appears to have been 'bantamised' to produce the miniature version. In turn, the miniature poodle was 'bred down' to produce the toy version.

What the dog may have lost in size, the toy poodle loses nothing in character, and retains the same lively personality and fiercely independent nature of its larger relatives. What it lacks in stature, the delightful toy poodle more than compensates for in affection, loyalty and its courageous spirit.

174

Pug

Other Names: **Carlin, mops**
Date of Origin: **Antiquity**
Place of Origin: **China**
Original Use: **Companion**
Modern Use: **Companion**
Size: Height: **10–11 in.**
Weight: **14–18 lb**
Colors: **Apricot, fawn, black, silver**
Recognized by: **A.K.C., K.C.**

The pug is often said to take its name from the Latin *pugnus* which means 'fist' – suggesting that the dog's profile resembles a clenched fist. The name pug, however, was not used until the late 18th century: today Latin countries still prefer to call these little dogs 'carlin'. An alternative theory for the name 'pug' is that the word was used in England to refer to pets in general, but to pet monkeys in particular! Like the name itself, the origins of the pug are also disputed: at one time the breed was thought to have come from Holland, but was in fact introduced there in the 16th century by traders with the Dutch East India Company. Today it is generally accepted to have originated in China, where miniaturized mastiffs were produced some 2,000 years ago. The pug arrived in Britain in 1688 when the court of William of Orange came to England. Originally, fawn was the most popular color – a color set

off most attractively by the black mask and dark, shining eyes. By the 18th century the pug had truly become a popular fashion accessory among the royal and the aristocratic set – so popular that even German and French porcelain factories made pug 'ornaments' which are now highly collectible, and valuable! The curled tail was delighted in, but the ears were cut off close to the head in the belief that the pain suffered by the pug would make the wrinkles on their faces deeper. Fortunately this practice is long gone.

Despite the breathing problems suffered by all breeds with 'flattened' faces – especially in hot summer months – the pug remains a very happy, tolerant, and good-natured breed. Sharing these fine qualities are pug owners – who have to endure their dog's quite tremendous snores!

Yorkshire Terrier

Other Names: **'Yorkies'**
Date of Origin: **19th century**
Place of Origin: **Great Britain**
Original Use: **Ratting**
Modern Use: **Companion**
Size: Height: **9 in.**
     Weight: **5–7 lb**
Colors: **Steel blue and rich tan in show dogs**
Recognized by: **A.K.C., K.C.**

One of the world's most instantly recognized breeds and one of the world's most popular too, the delightful Yorkie originated in the early 19th century in the West Riding of Yorkshire. They were bred by miners who wanted a terrier who was good at ratting but small enough to be carried in their pockets! The Yorkie is most likely the result of crosses between early black-and-tan terriers, Paisley and Clydesdale terriers. Originally Yorkies were somewhat larger dogs: but wise Yorkshire miners soon realized they could 'make a few bob' by selling the smaller, 'prettier' animals to their bosses! Soon size and quality were being refined further through selective breeding.

As a show dog, the Yorkie betrays nothing of this tough origin: its long silky coat sweeps the ground like a glossy curtain: they are brushed with the softest of brushes, bathed and oiled to keep them in the finest condition, and rolled up neatly in little protective bandaged bundles so the Yorkie can play without spoiling its hairdo! Even pet Yorkies are inevitably pampered and spoiled – and wear at least one little ribbon! Nevertheless, underneath it all, Yorkies are true terriers: tenacious and stubborn, they are veritable dynamos of energy, and possess some of the fastest little legs on any dog! And, if there were medals for 'yapping', some Yorkies would be world champions!

ST. BERNARD

Utility Dogs

The group system used to 'organize' the various breeds is largely arbitrary, as some dogs can fit easily into more than one category. In fact, it is possible to divide the breeds into any kind of category, for example, according to type, which would allow spitz-type dogs to be grouped together or the 'giant' breeds like the Newfoundland and St. Bernard to be grouped together. But it would be equally reasonable to group together curly-haired dogs, or long-haired dogs or wire-haired dogs, or to class short, long or tall dogs together!

The British group system, which is pretty closely followed by Commonwealth countries, is also substantially similar to the system adopted by North, Central and South American countries. The only real differences are in the naming of groups and the British tendency to include toy or miniature varieties in the same group in which the standard-sized dogs appear.

The toy, terrier, hound, and working dog groups are named the same in the U.S.A. and Britain. The gun dog group in the U.S.A. is known as the sporting group, while the utility group is known in the U.S.A. as the nonsporting group. Within these groups, the breeds are pretty much the same, but with the following notable exceptions:

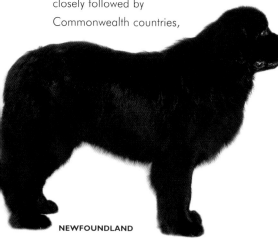

NEWFOUNDLAND

GERMAN SPITZ

POODLE

In Britain, all three varieties of the schnauzer are grouped in the utility group (in the U.S.A., they are split between the terrier group and working group).

Toy poodles in Britain are also kept with the other varieties in the utility group (instead of being placed with the toys as they are in North America).

Shih-tzus and lhasa apsos are included in the utility group in Great Britain (instead of being placed with the toys as they are in the U.S.A. – although not in Canada!).

The utility group is a 'catchall' group for breeds which do not fit 'exactly' into the other groups. Some choose to call utility dogs 'special dogs' and certainly some of them are unusual and unfamiliar breeds. Many of these dogs, however, are ancient breeds that were developed for a particular purpose or occupation, but which since that time, they have left behind. Two fine examples are the Dalmatian and the poodle: the former was a 'carriage dog' bred to trot alongside

coaches and carriages, simply to demonstrate the wealth and status of the carriage owner. The poodle is descended from German gun dogs and was once used as a water retriever and guard of herds. Today, although still feisty and still very brave, the poodle is almost exclusively a companion dog.

DALMATIAN

Boston Terrier

Other Names: **Boston bull**
Date of Origin: **19th century**
Place of Origin: **United States of America**
Original Use: **Fighting, ratting**
Modern Use: **Companion**
Size: Height: **15–17 in.**
      Weight: **10–25 lb**
Colors: **Black-brindle, red-brindle**
Recognized by: **A.K.C., K.C.**

The Boston terrier is one of many breeds and varieties developed in the United States, and is one of the most popular breeds in the country (for many, it is the 'national dog' of the U.S.A. It often comes as surprise that the well-mannered, considerate, spry and entertaining Boston terrier, which today is a delightful companion dog, was used in pit fighting in the Boston area. Bulldogs (see page180) and bull terriers (see page 217) were crossed with boxers (see page 146) and the now extinct white terrier to produce dogs with 'improved' fighting qualities.

Common practice was to name the dog after its owner and the name would then change as the dog was passed to a new owner: for example, the dog would be known as O'Toole's Bob, but when passed to a new owner would become Smith's Bob. The known history of the Boston terrier breed begins in 1870 when a dog of uncertain ancestry, was brought from England. This dog passed through several owners before ending up, in 1875, with one Robert C. Hooper, and the dog was thereafter known as Hooper's Judge.

Early dogs like Hooper's Judge weighed over 44 lb, so were closer to bulldog than terrier type. Later breeders bred the Boston down in size – both in body size and in head size – while still managing to retain the dog's unique looks, including its delightful 'bat ears'. Nevertheless, many Boston terriers still have a proportionally large head, and caesarean operations are often required to deliver pups as their heads are too large to pass through the mother's cervix. Three sizes exist in its native America: under 15 lb; 15-20 lb, and over 20 lb.

Bulldog

Other Names: **English bulldog, British bulldog**
Date of Origin: **19th century**
Place of Origin: **Great Britain**
Original Use: **Bull baiting**
Modern Use: **Companion**
Size: Height: **12–14 in.**
    Weight: **50–55 lb**
Colors: **Variety**
Recognized by: **A.K.C., K.C.**

Widely recognized as the symbol of courage and tenacity – a legacy of its bloodthirsty past as a fighting dog in bull pits – the thickset, heavily boned and 'low-slung' bulldog today is far removed in both looks and temperament from its early ancestors. The first mention of the 'bulldog' as a distinct breed occurs in 1631 in a letter from Prestwick Eaton to George Wellington asking for a mastiff and two 'good bulldogs'. At this time, bulldogs used for bull baiting looked more like Staffordshire bull terriers.

When bull baiting was made illegal in 1835 the breed was in danger of extinction and one breeder, Bill George worked to transform the bulldog into its present form, eliminating the ferocity of the breed. Unmistakable in appearance with its exaggerated shape, stout, strong front legs

firmly set, and planted wide apart on the ground, and the distinctive, wrinkled head, the bulldog is one of those breeds that people either love or hate on account of its appearance. Few can truly criticize the bulldog, though, for its temperament: it is one of the most amiable, dependable and good-natured breeds.

Despite its essential 'Britishness', the English bulldog has influenced a number of other breeds such as the boxer (see page 217), the Boston terrier (see page 179), the French bulldog (see page 181), the bull terrier and bull mastiff.

French Bulldog

To the horror of many British bulldog breeders, in 1898, a French version – daring to use the appellation 'bulldog' was shown in England! The bulldog was regarded as quintessentially British and although, its blood can be seen in other breeds such as the Boston terrier (see page 179), only the French dared to use the word! Some commentators in the 19th century even went so far to dispute the relationship between the two breeds and suggested that the Frenchie was in fact a descendant of the *dogue de burgos*, a Spanish bull-baiting dog. Nevertheless, the truth is that the little Frenchie is descended from the 'bantam' or miniaturized bulldogs bred in the 19th century in England. Many of these dogs were exported to France where they were crossed with French terriers and their offspring were used for rat hunting before becoming both companion dogs and something of a fashion accessory among the working classes in Paris.

Little beyond reducing the bulldog in size had actually been achieved in Europe, so it was left to breeders in the United States to improve and standardize the breed, especially the Frenchie's most distinctive feature – its delightful 'bat ears' which are natural to the breed and not cropped. It

Other Names: **Bouledogue Français, Frenchie**
Date of Origin: **19th century**
Place of Origin: **France**
Original Use: **Bull baiting**
Modern Use: **Companion**
Size: Height: **12 in.**
    Weight: **22–28 lb**
Colors: **Pied, black-brindle, red-brindle, fawn**
Recognized by: **A.K.C., K.C.**

was also in the United States that the Frenchie was first recognized as a distinct breed. The 'brutish' appearance is once again deceptive: underneath that often grumpy looking face lies a dog that is charming and playful, small enough to adapt well to urban life, peaceful, yet alert to strangers, and with a smooth lustrous coat that requires little grooming. It no surprise that the French Bulldog is such a popular dog.

Chow-chow

Other Names: None
Date of Origin: Antiquity
Place of Origin: China
Original Use: Food, draught animal, guarding
Modern Use: Companion
Size: Height: 18–22 in.
     Weight: 45–70 lb
Colors: Black, blue, cream-white, fawn, red
Recognized by: A.K.C., K.C.

The chow-chow has a rather 'unpalatable' history: in Manchuria and Mongolia, it was bred for human consumption, while its coat was used as fur trimming on clothing. Despite the fact that the meat was considered a great delicacy, the name chow-chow does not in fact come from the Cantonese-Chinese word for 'food', nor is it derived from the American cowboys' use of the word 'chow' for food.

In the 18th century, British sailors named the dogs chow-chow because these were the words they used to describe miscellaneous ships' cargo. An equivalent English word would have meant that the chow-chow would have been called 'ballast'!

The exact origins of the chow-chow remain a mystery: it is however, a spitz-type dog – a dog from the Arctic Circle and therefore a member of the same family as the Samoyed (see page 209), the Elkhound (see page 111), the 'husky' dogs, and the smallest of the spitz dogs, the Pomeranian (see page 172). It is likely that the chow-chow is the result of unions between some of these breeds and, perhaps, with some of the eastern mastiffs. Like many other spitz dogs, the chow-chow was used as a draft animal, pulling carts and sleds.

The first chow-chows are reputed to have arrived in England in 1780 where their unique black-blue tongue (and inside of the mouth) was noticed. No other canine has such a feature. They also appear to have rather small, and rather 'catlike' feet, are known for their independent streak.

Dalmatian

Other Names: **None official, but plenty of nicknames including: spotty dogs, firehouse dogs, dally**
Date of Origin: **Middle Ages**
Place of Origin: **Balkans, by way of India**
Original Use: **Carriage dog, hunting**
Modern Use: **Companion**
Size: Height: **20–24 in.**
Weight: **50–55 lb**
Colors: **White-black, white-liver**
Recognized by: **A.K.C., K.C.**

Although the breed takes its name from Dalmatia, on the eastern coast of the Adriatic Sea, there is evidence to suggest that these dogs originated first in northern India and were then taken to Greece: ancient Greek friezes dating from some 4,000 years old show hunting dogs that are similar to the Dalmatian. From Greece it is widely thought that the breed was taken to Dalmatia by gypsies, where they were used to warn of invasion by Ottoman Turkish forces.

By the 17th century, the Dalmatian was evident in western Europe: it seems that the wealthy brought many such dogs home with them as 'holiday souvenirs' from their Grand Tours of Europe. Dutch paintings show the dogs as both household companions and as hunting dogs, while in England, they were put to work as 'carriage dogs'. The Dalmatian was part of the English 'milord's' ostentatious display of wealth and was required to trot with the carriage. Sometimes the dogs worked at the sides of carriages, others were specially trained to trot in front of the lead horse, clearing the road in front and announcing the impeding arrival of someone very important. The finest display, however, was considered to be when the Dalmatian trotted under the poles, between two horses!

Because it worked with horses, the Dalmatian often shared the stables with them, and it proved itself a very capable vermin hunter. Its almost insatiable love of exercise and its familiarity with horses is probably how the Dalmatian became associated with fire engines. With the advent of motorized vehicles, the role of carriage dog ended, but the dallie remained the 'mascot' at many fire houses, especially in the U.S.A.

German Spitz

Other Names: Deutscher spitz (gross, mittel and klein) Deutscher gross spitz also known as wolf spitz.

Date of Origin: 17th century

Place of Origin: Germany

Original Use: Companion (gross and klein), farm work (mittel)

Modern Use: Companion (gross, mittel and klein)

Size: Height: Gross: 16 in.

Weight: Gross: 38½–40 lb

Mittel: 11½–14 in.; 13–41 lb

Klein: 9–11 in.; 18–22 lb

Colors: Gross: white, brown, black; mittel & klein: variety of colors

Recognized by: F.C.I.: gross; K.C.: mittel and klein

The German spitz occurs in three sizes: *gross* (large), *mittel* (medium or standard) and *klein* (little, or toy). The *gross* and *klein* varieties have always been companion dogs, while the *mittel* was an efficient herding dog on farms. The breed is most likely descended from the spitz-type dogs of the Arctic Circle, which arrived in Europe with the Viking invasions. The large German spitz, or 'wolf spitz' was known in Germany in 1450 and it is said that the white dogs were from Pomerania and the black dogs from Württemberg. When the German Spitz Club was formed in 1899, the large spitz averaged 17 in. at the shoulder, while the tallest of the small variety was a mere 11 in. tall at the shoulder.

The three types of German spitz are similar in conformation: the ears are compact and triangular, set high on the head and close together; the eyes appear large in proportion to the head; the small feet have insulating hair between the toes; the tail, covered in long hair, lies against the side of the body, and the chest is covered in dense, long, rather harsh hair.

The three varieties differ only in size, and in color: the gross occurs in white, black and brown, while the smaller dogs occur in a wider variety of colors. Their glorious coats require a great deal of attention but many of the dogs do resent this! Furthermore, they are not the easiest of breeds to obedience-train. Yet they are magnificent dogs and deserve greater and more widespread popularity than they currently enjoy.

German Pinscher

Other Names: **Standard pinscher**
Date of Origin: **18th century**
Place of Origin: **Germany**
Original Use: **Vermin control**
Modern Use: **Companion**
Size: Height: **16–19 in.**
　　　Weight: **25–35 lb**
Colors: **Dark brown, black–tan, fawn**
Recognized by: **A.K.C., K.C.**

Among Germany's contribution to the terrier breed are the famous schnauzer (see page 188) and the affenpinscher (see page 151) – although in England, the schnauzer (in all three varieties) is placed in the utility (non-sporting) group, and the affenpinscher, on account of its size, is grouped with other toy breeds.

Pinscher is the German word for 'biter' – or 'terrier' – and the German pinscher, or standard pinscher, is now quite a rare breed, being overtaken in the popularity stakes by the miniature pinscher (see page169), which is a terrier and an equally ancient breed, (but which is placed in the toy group) and the relatively modern Doberman pinscher, which is classed in the working group (see page 248). The German pinscher played a pivotal role in developing both the 'min pin' and the Doberman. A tall terrier, the German pinscher was the archetypal multipurpose farm dog: it would chase and kill rabbits, rats, and other vermin, it guarded and drove livestock and it

made an ideal watchdog on remote country farms. While it is still used in country areas as a watchdog, the German pinscher responds quite well to obedience-training and can, in the hands of an experienced and responsible owner, be a loyal companion dog.

The German pinscher is a medium-sized dog with a well-muscled body and a short, smooth and glossy coat. The long muzzle ends in a blunt tip with a black nose. In countries which prohibit ear cropping, these pinschers have triangular shaped ears with a natural, half fold. Coupled with their dark, oval eyes, they have a very attractive expression. When the ears are cropped, however, the Pinscher appears, at first sight, a much more ferocious dog.

Schnauzer (Giant, standard and miniature)

Other Names: Giant schnauzer: Riesenschnauzer, Münchener dog

Standard Schnauzer: Mittelschnauzer, miniature schnauzer: Zwergschnuazer

Date of Origin: Middle Ages (giant & standard), 15th century (miniature)

Place of Origin: Germany

Original Use: Cattle herding (giant); ratting, guarding (standard); ratting (miniature)

Modern Use: Companion (giant, standard & miniature), service dogs (giant)

Size: Height: Giant: 23½– 27½ in.
Weight: 70–77 lb

Standard: 18–20 in.; 32–34 lb

Miniature: 12–14 in.; 13–15 lb

Colors: Giant & standard: Pepper–salt, black

Miniature: Black–silver, pepper–salt, black

Recognized by: A.K.C., K.C.

The name 'schnauzer' comes from *Schnauze* the German word for snout, nose, or muzzle. A second word, *Schnauzbart,* means moustache. All three breeds of schnauzers are conspicuous by their moustaches and beards – which do make them look like very dignified gentlemen.

The most powerful of all the schnauzers, the giant or *Riesenschnauzer,* as it is known in Germany today, hails from the south of Bavaria, near to Swabia where it was used as a cattle and drover's dog. When the need of farmers for this type of dog declined, in the 19th century, the Riesenschnauzer became associated with brewers and butchers, who were no doubt more able to feed the dog well! For these owners, the Riesenschnauzer now had a new role as a guard dog and it was this

ability that led the giant schnauzer into service in both the police and the military.

The giant schnauzer bears a strong resemblance to another drover's dog, the bouvier des Flandres, although there is no evidence to show that they are in fact related. The dog seems to have been developed by increasing the size of the *Mittelschnauzer* (standard schnauzer).

The first appearance of the giant schnauzer in a dog show was in Munich in 1909 where it was called the 'Russian Bear Schnauzer' and they created such a sensation that the Munich Schnauzer Club was formed almost immediately.

The origins of the *Mittleschnauzer* are also obscure, but it does seem to be the oldest of the three breeds: In Stuttgart, Germany, there is a statue of a watchman and a dog which has the characteristics of the *Mittelschnauzer*. Furthermore, the German artist, Albrecht Dürer (1471–1528), had a similar dog, whose image he painted several times between 1490 and 1504. Some claim the standard was the result of crosses in the Middle Ages between two now long extinct breeds, others claim it evolved from crosses of the

(extinct) *Schäferpudel* and the wire-haired German pinscher – which led to it being called the schnauzer–pinscher for a time.

It seems likely that like the *Riesenschnauzer*, the *Mittelschnauzer* originated in the cattle- and sheep-herding areas of southern Germany, particularly in Bavaria and Württemberg, where it was highly regarded both as a cattle dog and as a ratter. The breed was first shown in Hanover, Germany, in 1879 and, the following year the breed standard was established. Today, the *Mittelschnauzer* is largely a companion dog, and one of the most popular breeds in both Britain and North America where it became well known after World War I.

The miniature, or *Zwergschnauzer*, is an almost perfect replica of the giant and standard schnauzer. It emerged about 1900 and, despite appearances, is not just a scaled down standard, but is the result of crosses between these and affenpinschers (see page 151) and possibly other miniature pinschers. In its early days the *Zwergschnauzer* was a renowned rat catcher – and killer. Today it is among the favorite companion dogs: easy to train, good with children and other dogs, a good barker and an enthusiastic guard dog.

189

Shiba Inu

Other Names: Japanese shiba inu
Date of Origin: Antiquity
Place of Origin: Japan
Original Use: Small game hunting
Modern Use: Companion
Size: Height: 14–16 in
       Weight: 18–22 lb
Colors: Variety
Recognized by: A.K.C., K.C.

The shiba inu is one of a number of spitz-type dogs native to Japan and the country's most popular breed – with a growing fan club in Australia, Europe and North America.

The spitz-type dogs that evolved in the Arctic Circle regions moved out of northeastern Asia into China and Korea some 4,000 years ago and became the foundation stock for today's chow-chow from China and the Jindo from Korea. Around 2,500 years ago, spitz-type dogs were taken to Japan – possibly from Korea – and these are believed to form the foundation stock of the Japanese spitz-type dogs such as the hokkaido, akita (see page 191), ainu dog, kai dog, shikoku and the shiba inu. (The Japanese spitz, however, is a much more recently developed breed.)

The shiba inu has existed in the Sanin region of Japan for thousands of years: bones dated at 2,500 years old have been found in archaeological excavations.

The shiba inu is the smallest of all the indigenous Japanese breeds – *shiba* means small – and, like the primitive basenji (see page 86), it does not bark but has a quite extraordinary shriek! A good-looking dog, with well-developed, strong legs, a deep chest, pointed muzzle and dark nose, and thick, strong tail, the shiba inu is set to become even more popular worldwide.

Akita

Japanese breeds are classified and named according to their size: *akita* (large), *shika* (medium) and *shiba* (small). There is, however, only one *akita* (large) breed and that is of course, the akita inu, which basically translates as 'large dog'! This spitz-type dog was once bred for fighting but when this sport declined, it was used for hunting wild boar, deer and the Japanese black bear, with ownership restricted to the highest classes in Japanese society.

By the 1930s, however, numbers of akitas had declined in Japan to near extinction: to make matters worse, the breed was completely unknown outside Japan. It was not until the American occupation in the late 1940s that the breed's powerful presence impressed the U.S. forces. Interest in preserving the breed grew, with the founding of the Society for the Preservation of Japanese Breeds in order to increase the population of indigenous breeds.

By nature, the akita is undemonstrative – its does seem more expressionless, and

Other Names: **Akita inu, Japanese akita,**
Date of Origin: **17th century**
Place of Origin: **Japan**
Original Use: **Large game hunting, fighting**
Modern Use: **Guard dog, companion**
Size: Height: **24–28 in.**
　　　Weight: **75–110 lb**
Colors: **Any colors**
Recognized by: **A.K.C., K.C.**

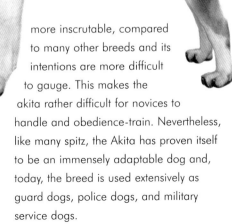

more inscrutable, compared to many other breeds and its intentions are more difficult to gauge. This makes the akita rather difficult for novices to handle and obedience-train. Nevertheless, like many spitz, the Akita has proven itself to be an immensely adaptable dog and, today, the breed is used extensively as guard dogs, police dogs, and military service dogs.

Japanese Spitz

Other Names: **None**
Date of Origin: **20th century**
Place of Origin: **Japan**
Original Use: **Companion**
Modern Use: **Companion, security**
Size: Height: **12–14 in.**
    Weight: **11–13 lb**
Colors: **White**
Recognized by: **A.K.C., K.C.**

The Japanese spitz is one of a number of small, white, fluffy breeds. This spitz is a classic example of miniaturisation: the Japanese spitz is half the size of its progenitor, the Samoyed (see page 209) which came from the most northerly regions of central Asia with the nomadic Samoyed tribe, from which it received its name, before being introduced to Japan. It is possible however, that another spitz breed – the Finnish spitz and the Norwegian buhund are possible contenders – contributed to the development of the Japanese spitz.

    The Japanese spitz is around

12 in. high, with a long, pure white coat, and a magnificent plumed tail. It also shares other common spitz characteristics: tough, lively, nimble, and bold. In the 1950s the Japanese spitz became immensely popular in its homeland but, since then, numbers have declined. In contrast, this fluffy 'snowball' of a dog has become enormously popular in the United States and in Europe, where it is both a companion animal and an effective home protector. In some instances, this little – but tough – breed has a successful life as a professional security dog.

Lhasa Apso

Other Names: **Apso seng kyi, Tibetan apso**
Date of Origin: **Antiquity**
Place of Origin: **Tibet**
Original Use: **Companion**
Modern Use: **Companion**
Size: Height: **10–11 in.**
      Weight: **13–15 lb**
Colors: **Bicolor, black, brown, white, golden, dark-grizzle**
Recognized by: **A.K.C., K.C.**

The lhasa apso is one of four Tibetan breeds, originally associated with the ancient monasteries of Tibet, where they were bred as companions for the monks and used as barking sentinels. Its bark is said to be the basis for the breed's name in Tibet: *apso seng kyi* translates as 'barking sentinel lion dog'. Others maintain that *apso* is a corruption of the word *rapso*, the Tibetan word for goat, and suggest that the breed was so named because its coat looked like those of the goats kept by local herdsmen.

These dogs were believed to bring good luck and, because of their association with the monasteries, to have a religious significance. Consequently, the breed was treated with the greatest of respect and it was considered an honor to be given one as a gift. The lhasa apso was common in the wealthy 'homes' of Tibet – the royal palaces and the palace of the Dalai Lama.

The first lhasa apso was seen in the West in 1921, but was initially grouped in one category with the shih-tzu (see page 198): the confusion may have been caused by the fact that both breeds were evident in Tibet. The Dalai Lama is known to have given palace-bred apsos as gifts to dignitaries, especially those of foreign countries. Consequently apsos went to China, where the Imperial Court practice was to offer shih-tzus – which are probably crosses between the Tibetan apsos and the Chinese Pekingese (see page 171) – as gifts in return. That's how the shih-tzu found its way to Tibet. In 1934, however, the lhasa apso and the shih-tzu were both recognized as distinct breeds. In the U.S.A., lhasa apsos are classed in the non-sporting dogs category.

Poodle (Standard and Miniature)

Other Names: Caniche, barbone

Date of Origin: Middle Ages (standard) 16th century (miniature)

Place of Origin: Germany (standard), France (miniature)

Original Use: Water retrieving (standard), companion (miniature)

Modern Use: Companion, security (standard)

Size: Height: Standard: 15 in.; miniature: 11–15 in.
Weight: Standard: 45–70 lb.; miniature: 26–30 lb

Colors: All solid colors

Recognized by: A.K.C., K.C.

One of the most popular companion breeds today, the poodle – in its standard size – was originally bred as a water retriever in Germany in the Middle Ages: its French name 'caniche' means 'duck dog' and the traditional method of clipping the coat with the hind quarters shaved – known in Europe as the 'lion trim' and in North America as the 'continental cut' – was to make it easier for the dog to swim and retrieve. Later, the little 'bobbles' of hair around the joints were left on to protect them from injury and from rheumatism. The hair on the head was also tied back – first with string and then with brightly colored ribbons, so the owners could distinguish their dog from others in the water.

miniaturisation can often bring with it a 'puppy-like' heightened dependence on people, most poodles inevitably retain their sparky independent personalities. Consequently, all the pleasures of owning a big dog are combined with the advantages of a small one! Likewise, miniatures and toys are all clipped for show in the same distinctive manner as the standards – although on the smaller dogs this probably takes a great deal less time! In Britain, the toy poodle is classified along with its larger relatives in the utility dogs category. In the U.S.A. it is classed as a toy.

The standard poodle was probably taken from Germany to France in the 16th century and, by this stage, it seems that the poodle had already been 'bantamized' to the reduced size of the miniature poodle, which in turn was used to produce the diminutive toy poodle. Both the miniature and toy poodles were, in the 1950s, the world's most popular dog and a much desired fashion accessory! The miniature poodle and toy poodle not only inherited the 'make and shape' of their 'big brother', but also their character: while

Schipperke

Other Names: 'Little skipper', 'little boatman', 'little captain'
Date of Origin: 16th century
Place of Origin: Belgium
Original Use: Small mammal hunting, barge guarding
Modern Use: Companion
Size: Height: 9–13 in.
　　　Weight: 7–18 lb
Colors: Black
Recognized by: A.K.C., K.C.

Another small, spitz-type dog, the small, jet-black, tailless schipperke, with its fox-like head and black nose and eyes, hails from Belgium. Its name translates as 'little skipper' or 'little captain' because this dog could be found working on the Flanders and Brabant canal boats, keeping down vermin and warning of any intruders. Schipperke enthusiasts claim that the two black dogs without tails, which are said to have rescued the Dutch prince, William of Orange, from assassins were schipperkes. If this is true, then the breed was well established during the prince's lifetime (1533–1584). One theory is that the schipperke is a small-sized descendant of a now-extinct Belgian sheepdog breed or of yet another extinct small breed, the leunvanaar.

Before 1700, however, craftsmen in the St. Gery area of Belgium were known to parade their black, tailless dogs on alternate Sundays, decorated with large brass collars in elaborate designs. These craftsmen didn't call the dogs schipperkes, but simply spitz. This gives rise to the theory that it in fact belongs to the breed of northern dogs, which originated in the Arctic Circle. Anatomically, it is a spitz-type dog and could therefore be related to other European breeds such as the Pomeranian (see page 172) or the German spitz.

Shar Pei

Other Names: Chinese fighting dog
Date of Origin: 16th century
Place of Origin: China
Original Use: Dog fighting, herding, hunting
Modern Use: Companion
Size: Height: 18–20 in.
Weight: 35–45 lb
Colors: Black, red, fawn, cream
Recognized by: A.K.C., K.C.

The unusual shar pei comes from China's southern province of Guangdong where it descended from mastiffs and spitz-type dogs, and was used as a fighting dog. It is indeed one of the more unusual dogs: the hard, prickly coat is oversized and wrinkled, and the hairs stand on end. The looseness and the texture were said to give the dog added protection during fights. The canine teeth are also curved like scimitars, making it very difficult for the dog to release the jaws once a hold has been established. The shar pei also has the blue-black tongue of another Chinese breed, the chow-chow (see page 182) which suggests there may be a link between the two breeds. This rather rather poetic Chinese description provides the best description: "Clamshell ears, butterfly nose, lion-shaped head, grandmother's face, water buffalo's neck, horse's buttocks and dragon's legs".

The shar pei was driven almost to extinction in China in the 20th century following the edict outlawing all dogs on the mainland. Some specimens were in Hong Kong, however, and from these, the breeder Matgo Law was able to successfully re-establish the breed, which was continued in the United States. When the shar pei first arrived in the West, it often suffered from severe eye problems which required surgical intervention. Successive breeding has reduced this problem but not, unfortunately, the high incidence of skin problems which trouble the breed. Frequent medicated shampooing of the dog's 'piggy bristle' coat is required – with special attention paid to its wrinkles. The shar pei has also suffered on account of its fighting past: they can be occasionally aggressive and are not suited to novice owners, but in the right hands they are calm and friendly dogs.

Shih-tzu

Other Names: **Chrysanthemum dog, lion dog**
Date of Origin: **17th century**
Place of Origin: **China**
Original Use: **Imperial Court dog**
Modern Use: **Companion**
Size: Height: **10–11 in.**
 Weight: **10–16 lb**
Colors: **Any colors**
Recognized by: **A.K.C., K.C.**

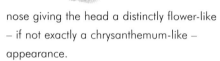

The shih-tzu – pronounced 'shid-zoo'
means 'lion dog' in Chinese. It was bred in
the imperial court of the Chinese emperors
and is thought to be a cross between the
Tibetan lhasa apso (see page 193) and the
ancestors of today's Pekingese (see page
171). The so-called 'lion dogs' were highly
prized in court circles: lions feature
prominently in Buddhist mythology and it
was believed that the Buddha himself kept
a lion as a pet. The prerevolutionary Peking
Kennel Club standard for the breed is
possibly the most poetic description of dog
ever: 'a lion head, bear torso, camel hoof,
feather-duster tail, palm-leaf ears, rice
teeth, pearly petal tongue and the
movement of a goldfish.'

Also known as the chrysanthemum dog,
this name is derived from the upward-
growing beard, whiskers and hair on the
nose giving the head a distinctly flower-like
– if not exactly a chrysanthemum-like –
appearance.

The first pair of shih-tzus was brought to
Britain from Peking by General Sir Gordon
Brownrigg as recently as 1930. More were
imported, but there were insufficient
numbers to gain a separate register until
1934. Until then, the shih-tzu was grouped
into one category with the lhasa apso and
the Tibetan terrier (see page 200). The
shih-tzu is less aloof and more playful in
character than its Tibetan cousin, and this
is enhanced by the dark, round eyes.
Probably because of their compact size,
shih-tzus are not classed as utility dogs
in the U.S.A., but are to be found in the
toy group.

Tibetan Spaniel

The Tibetan spaniel is a spaniel in name only: this breed was never developed to hunt but was trained to turn the prayer wheels of the Buddhist monks in the monasteries of Tibet. Legend has it that the breed was an ancient one – dating back to the time before written recorded history. Certainly the breed is old, as there is no recorded history of Tibet itself until the 7th century. As the early history of Tibet is linked with China, the custom of giving small dogs as diplomatic gifts may have led to the Tibetan spaniel arriving in China where it was crossed with pugs (see page 175) to produce 'Pekes' (see page 171).

Other Names: **None**
Date of Origin: **Tibet**
Place of Origin: **Antiquity**
Original Use: **Monk's companion dog**
Modern Use: **Companion**
Size: Height: **10 in.**
    Weight: **9–15 lb**
Colors: **Any colors**
Recognized by: **A.K.C., K.C.**

An alternative theory is that Pekes were gifts from China to Tibet, where they lost their breed purity over the centuries to form the Tibetan spaniel. The Peke and the Tibetan spaniel are anatomically similar, although the latter is longer in the leg and longer-faced – which gives it fewer respiratory problems than the Pekingese.

The first known Tibetan spaniel was brought to Britain by a Mr. F. Wormald in 1905. In the 1920s a medical missionary, Dr. Grieg, brought more dogs back to England, but the establishment of the breed in Britain really had to wait until after World War II when Sir Edward and Lady Wakefield's pair called Lama and Dolma founded the breed known today.

Tibetan Terrier

Other Names: **Dhoki apso, double chrysanthemum dog**
Date of Origin: **Middle Ages**
Place of Origin: **Tibet**
Original Use: **Guarding**
Modern Use: **Companion**
Size: Height: **14–16 in.**
 Weight: **18–30 lb**
Colors: **Variety of colors**
Recognized by: **A.K.C., K.C.**

As the Tibetan spaniel is not a true spaniel, the Tibetan terrier is not a true terrier: it was never bred to 'go to earth' but instead was used as a companion and very vocal guard dog by its Buddhist monk owners. For this reason, in the UK, the Tibetan terrier is not included in terrier group, but in the utility group. The breed is said to be very ancient and dogs were given as gifts by the monks to nomadic tribes as good luck mascots. These tribes seem to have used the dogs for guarding and herding flocks.

The Tibetan terrier is quite a small dog but it is well muscled. The body and head are a little like a miniature version of an Old English sheepdog (see page 236) – but the tail is quite different. The Tibetan's tail is magnificently plumed, curled, and carried elegantly over the back. The 'bangs' or fringes of hair at each end – over the eyes and over the rump of the dog – earned it the nickname of the 'double chrysanthemum dog'. The long coat, which is clipped in hot summer weather, was traditionally woven with yak hair to produce a soft, semi-waterproof cloth. Coat color was therefore important: pure black and pure white being the most highly prized colors. The Tibetan terrier is also presumed to be the only breed in the world required to have large flat feet – although these are hidden under a profusion of fine, long hairs.

Working Dogs

The working group is the largest and is made up of those breeds of dogs which serve man's needs: guard dogs, sledge dogs, herding dogs, and drovers (generally referred to as pastoral dogs), rescue and tracker dogs, guide dogs and general helpers, as well as those breeds which, at one time, were used as draft animals. It is often found that many of the breeds included in the working dog group possess a variety of skills.

Dogs were established as the hunting companions of humans well before man began to domesticate other animals such as cattle, horses and sheep. Domestication of livestock only began around 1,000 BC. Farmers had no use for hunting dogs and regarded these with the utmost suspicion since they could easily prey on their valuable herds. What were needed were dogs that would guard the flocks from predators and dogs that would round up herds without attacking the animals. 'Pastoral' dogs are interesting in that they have an natural instinct to run 'with the pack' – except that the pack is a group of animals that are not dogs – and have no desire to injure or kill their 'quarry'. What seems to have occurred in pastoral dogs is that the dog's natural instinct to be the pack leader, or 'top dog' has been exploited and developed through breeding and training.

SWEDISH VALLHUND

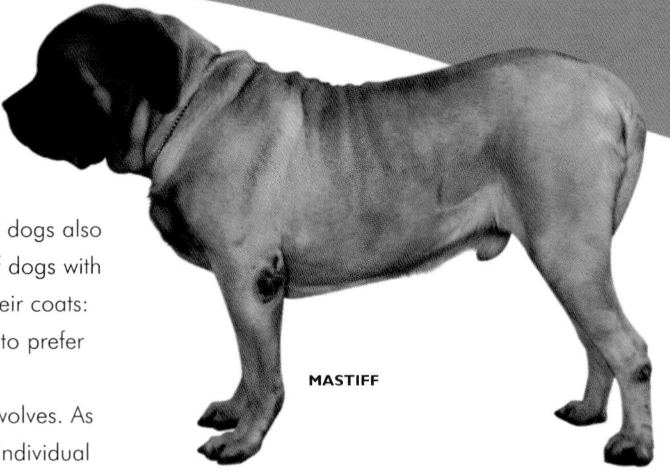

MASTIFF

Selective breeding of pastoral dogs also encouraged the development of dogs with larger proportions of white in their coats: farmers and shepherds seemed to prefer this, as it made the dogs more distinguishable from predatory wolves. As herd sizes increased over time, individual animals had to be prevented from straying: small, fast, agile dogs were needed to move strays back to the herds, and these dogs became the herding dogs. When herds were required to be moved en masse over sometimes quite considerable, distances – to markets or to new pastures – another type of dog was required, the drover. The Old English sheepdog (see page 236), the corgi (see page 245) and the Swedish Vallhund (see page 211) were all cattle droving dogs. These protected and drove the herds along. Large, bulky dogs were needed for livestock such as cattle, while smaller drover dogs were used to move sheep and goats. These became the

forerunners of the modern sheepdog.

Some other breeds that we don't readily associate with pastoral duties include mastiffs. Used as a weapon of war, the mastiffs were also employed to protect and herd the flocks of animals that were required to accompany (and to feed) armies on the move. Many of today's mountain dogs are descended from

HUSKY

ALASKAN MALAMUTE

mastiffs: their large size is a legacy of this ancestry of ancient 'war dogs'. As the mastiffs moved across Europe and Asia with conquering armies and traders, they bred with the spitz-type dogs of northern regions and left their legacy in breeds such as the shar pei (see page 197).

The 'husky' type dogs, or sled dogs of the Arctic Circle are also included in the working group. These were used not only to pull sleds across winter snows, but as pack animals in summer months. Many of these dogs, such as the Alaskan malamute and Siberian huskies, still take part in sled races. Teams from across the world compete at the World Championships. Held annually at Anchorage, Alaska, and

race over three 25-mile dashes held on consecutive days. Drivers may start with any number of dogs in the team, but they must finish each day with the same number – even if they have to ride home one of the sledges themselves! The most famous dog-sledge race from Nenana to Nome, Alaska, in January 1925, was not against other dog teams, but against diphtheria: the Alaskan winter had cut off rail and air links to Nome when the disease struck. Antitoxin was dispatched from Nenana and transported to Nome – a distance overland of 680 miles – by 20 relays of dog teams in just 127 ½ hours – that's just over five days at an average of 136 miles (220 km) a day.

203

Canaan

Other Names: **Kelef k'naani**
Date of Origin: **Antiquity**
Place of Origin: **Middle East**
Original Use: **Pariah–scavenger dog**
Modern Use: **Livestock guarding/herding, tracking/search & rescue, companion**
Size: Height: **19–24 in.**
       Weight: **35–55 lb**
Colors: **Black, brown, sand, white**
Recognized by: **A.K.C., K.C.**

As wandering groups of people spread out of southwest Asia around 15,000 years ago, 'canny canines' followed them. Pariah, or scavenging dogs, realized that if they 'hung around' humans long enough, there would be edible morsels at hand without having to hunt for them. As self–appointed guard dogs, many would become domesticated. The Canaan dog is one such primitive dog that has existed in the Middle East for thousands of years. Originally a pariah, it then became used by the nomadic Bedouin in the Negev Desert as a guard dog and herder. The breed was developed in the 1930s by Dr. Rudolphina Menzel, who conducted a selective breeding program in Jerusalem. During World War II a number of Canaans were successfully trained to detect land mines and after the war, some were trained as guide dogs for the blind.

In the region today, the Canaan is still used for herding, but its keen senses have also earned it recognition as a search and rescue dog. A medium-sized, very robust dog, the Canaan's coat is straight and harsh. Its most distinguishing feature is the bushy tail, which when the dog is alert, curls up and over the back.

Alaskan Malamute

Other Names: **Mahlemut**
Date of Origin: **Antiquity**
Place of Origin: **North America**
Original Use: **Sled pulling, hunting**
Modern Use: **Companion, sled pulling/sled racing**
Size: Height: **23–28 in.**
  Weight: **85–112 lb**
Colors: **Various shades of gray with black cap or mask**
Recognized by: **A.K.C., K.C.**

Wolf-like in appearance, the Alaskan malamute is named after the Mahlemut Inuit living on the Kotsebue Sound, on the Arctic coast of western Alaska. The Mahlemuts lived in a fishing and hunting environment, since behind the coast line lies mountainous territory. The Alaskan malamute is the largest of the sled-dog breeds and is strong enough to haul heavily loaded sleds over difficult terrain. Single dogs were used to haul a *travois* – a simple platform made by lashing together two poles – while a team of dogs could haul a half-ton.

The Inuit often boasted that these dogs were pure-bred tamed wolves, or the result of tamed wolf-dog crosses: while it seems likely that crosses did take place, it was with other dogs than wolves, especially other spitz-type dogs of the Arctic Circle region. The malamute was not only a sled dog; in summer when sleds couldn't be used, the dogs carried packs strapped under their bellies. The immense physical strength of the dogs was such that some were able to carry 50 lb packs up to 20 miles every day.

The pure-bred malamute dogs could not, however, withstand the onslaught of the Yukon gold rush. Haulage dogs were in such great demand, that animals of all types were shipped into the region and the result was numerous crossbreeding and a distillation of the bloodline. Fortunately enough, malamutes survived to recommence a breeding program and Canadian and American breeders began to show them in the 1940s.

Finnish Lapphund

Other Names: Lapinkoira, Lapland dog
Date of Origin: 17th century
Place of Origin: Finland
Original Use: Reindeer herding
Modern Use: Herding, companion
Size: Height : 18–20½ in.
    Weight: 44–47 lb
Colors: Variety
Recognized by: A.K.C., K.C.

The lapinkoira, or Finnish lapphund, is the traditional and historic herding dog of the Sami people. Used for herding reindeer – though today it is mostly to be found herding cattle and sheep – the Finnish lapphund is the result of interbreeding between the spitz-type dogs of the northern regions and the herding dogs from further south in Europe. Semi-domesticated reindeer were bred across Scandinavia and when interest in indigenous cultures – and indigenous dogs – developed, the Swedes and the Finns claimed the breed as their own. Two avoid any problems, two breeds were recognized internationally: the Finnish lapphund or lapinkoira and the Swedish lapphund or lapland spitz. In essence, these dogs are one breed but in two countries.

Selective breeding procedures in Finland have maintained the Finnish lapphund's herding instincts but, outside of the country, they are often to be found as companions and well-loved house pets. In many instances, the 'pet' animals have been developed for looks rather than function: their herding instincts have been diminished in favor of a more luxuriously dense and colored coat which, along with their curled tail, makes them extremely attractive.

Siberian Husky

The origin of the word 'husky' is hotly debated: some claim the word derives from the Chukchi or Chuchi Inuit people of the Koyma River region in Siberia; others, that it is derived from the Tuski or Tschutski nomadic tribes who herded domesticated reindeer and were described by William Hulme Hooper of the British Royal Navy, who spent ten months with the tribe in 1853. Hooper described the dogs of this tribe as small and wiry, and the sleds they pulled as constructed for speed rather than weight, and without reins, but by command of the owner's voice alone.

Other Names: Arctic Husky
Date of Origin: Antiquity
Place of Origin: Siberia
Original Use: Sled pulling
Modern Use: Companion, sled racing
Size: Height: 20–23½ in.
       Weight: 35–60 lb
Colors: Any colors
Recognized by: A.K.C., K.C.

Whatever the exact origins of the name, it has since spread across the Arctic regions and come to mean 'sled dogs' in general. However, the Siberian variety is the only dog to be officially registered as a husky. It is also one of the few breeds to have blue, brown, hazel or non-solid colored eyes, but, in common with other spitz-type dogs, the Siberian husky seldom barks – but does, like wolves, join in heartily with the communal howling 'songs'!

It was the Yukon gold rush that focused attention onto sled dogs, and drivers of teams were proud of their animals, their skill and endurance. Rivalry was expressed in racing, including the famous All-Alaska Sweepstakes covering some 408 miles. In 1909 the fleet-footed dogs of the Chukchi raced for the first time under the name Siberian huskies and, in the following years, were among the winners. In 1948 a team of Siberian huskies raced a measured 10 mile-course in a mere 35 minutes.

Samoyed

The Samoyed is a spitz breed which takes it name from the Siberian nomadic tribe of the Samoyedes. The breed was largely unknown until explorers in the 18th century noticed how they were highly valued by their owners who used the dogs to haul sleds, herd reindeer and guard the yurts (the tents) of their owners, and how their hair was used for spinning and weaving into clothes! The first Samoyedes, as they were then called, were brought to western Europe in 1889 by fur traders who travelled far north into Russia and Siberia to buy sables. The first dogs were used also as sled dogs: Fridtjof Nansen, the Norwegian explorer used Samoyeds on his first polar expedition (1893–96) and, later, Captain Scott also used the breed on his second attempt to reach the South Pole.

In their native lands, Samoyeds could be a variety of shades including black, and black and tan, but once they reached Britain in 1900, breeders favored the pure white-, biscuit-and-cream-colored dogs and eventually the breed standard was

Other Names: **Samoyedskaya**
Date of Origin: **Antiquity**
Place of Origin: **Russia**
Original Use: **Reindeer herding**
Modern Use: **Companion**
Size: Height: **18–22 in.**
Weight: **50–66 lb**
Colors: **White, white-biscuit, cream**
Recognized by: **A.K.C., K.C.**

limited to these. Affectionate and lively – but also known to be a little noisy and sometimes aggressive with other dogs – the most delightful characteristic of the breed is that it always appears to be smiling! The black lips have an upward curl and, when coupled with sparkling brown eyes, it is very easy to forgive the Samoyed for not being the easiest breed to obedience-train!

Norwegian Buhund

Other Names: Norsk buhund, Norwegian sheepdog
Date of Origin: Antiquity
Place of Origin: Norway
Original Use: Sheep/cattle herding, guarding
Modern Use: Herding, farm/livestock guarding, companion
Size: Height: 16–18 in.
      Weight: 53–58 lb
Colors: Wheaten, black, red
Recognized by: K.C.

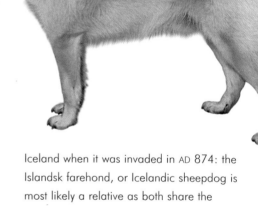

Fearless and energetic, the Norwegian buhund is a 'jack-of-all-trades': once used to pull sleds and to accompany hunters, on remote farmsteads it could also be found herding ponies and cattle and acting as a guard dog. *Bu* in Norwegian means 'shed' or 'stall,' and refers to the breed's later work around domesticated livestock. Such is its herding instinct that the buhund has recently found popularity in Australia as a sheepdog. Although a spitz-type dog of the type that originated in the intensely cold regions of the Arctic Circle, the Norwegian buhund seems to thrive in the heat of Australia.

The antipodes is not the only port of call for these well-travelled dogs: the buhund is said to have sailed with the Vikings and, almost certainly, it accompanied them to Iceland when it was invaded in AD 874: the Islandsk farehond, or Icelandic sheepdog is most likely a relative as both share the distinctive high-set curly tail.

Some describe the buhund as a rather 'plain-looking' dun-colored dog, but this is far from the truth. The colors are a beautiful wheaten shading to pearly white or they can be red, or even a beautiful black. The lighter-colored dogs have an attractive 'smudge' of black on the muzzle and ears, and all have lovely bright, dark brown eyes, outlined by dark eyelids.

Swedish Vallhund

Other Names: **Vollhund, vasgotaspets, Swedish cattle dog**
Date of Origin: **Middle Ages**
Place of Origin: **Sweden**
Original Use: **Cattle herding/droving, guarding, ratting**
Modern Use: **Herding, guarding, ratting, companion**
Size: Height: **12–14 in.**
      Weight: **25–35 lb**
Colors: **Gray, gray-brown, red-brown, red-yellow**
Recognized by: **K.C.**

Classified in Sweden as an indigenous breed, the once rare, short, yet powerfully legged Swedish Vallhund, like the Pembroke corgi which it resembles, is descended from the European bassets: some say that corgis were taken to Scandinavia by the Vikings on their return from invading Wales. In Sweden the Vallhund was an 'all-purpose' farm dog: herding and driving cattle, guarding farms and livestock and working as a pest controller, keeping down vermin in the hay and straw barns. Used widely but little considered, it was suddenly realized in the 1940s that the Swedish Vallhund was on the verge of extinction. Fortunately, the breed was rescued and revived by Swedish breeder von Rosen, with official recognition awarded by the Swedish Kennel Club, and the numbers are secure once more. In Sweden it can still be found working on farms, but increasingly it is being seen in both the show ring and in homes as a companion dog.

211

Mastiff

Other Names: **English mastiff**
Date of Origin: **Antiquity**
Place of Origin: **Great Britain**
Original Use: **Guarding**
Modern Use: **Guarding, companion**
Size: Height: **27 ½–30 in.**
      Weight: **175–190 lb**
Colors: **Apricot-fawn, silver-fawn, dark fawn-brindle**
Recognized by: **A.K.C., K.C.**

In the years before kennel clubs and pedigree registers it was common to call any large dog a mastiff – including Saint Bernards and Newfoundlands! Today, only a handful of breeds are properly called mastiffs: the English mastiff (known around the world simply as the mastiff); the Japanese tosa inu, the Tibetan mastiff (see page 214), and the Neapolitan mastiff (see page 213). Other dogs do have the name mastiff as well, such as the Spanish, Brazilian, Sicilian and Pyrenean mastiffs, These may well have mastiff ancestry, but they are not 'true' mastiffs and are largely recognized only by the F.C.I. under these names.

One of the heaviest dog breeds in existence, the mastiff existed in Assyria around 700 BC and was perhaps brought to Britain by Phoenician traders. These huge dogs were fighting alongside the ancient Britons when the Romans invaded Britain. They were so impressed by their size and courage that they sent many mastiffs back to Rome to fight in the 'circus' – the arenas – against lion, bulls, bears, tigers, and even gladiators. These fighting qualities have been tied to the breed ever since, although they were also known later in England as 'band dogges' and 'tie dogges', terms used to describe guard dogs. The word mastiff is thought to be derived from the Anglo-Saxon word *masty*, meaning 'powerful'.

Breeding – and housing – such large breeds is nothing short of a challenge and all breeds, but especially the larger ones, tend to suffer: by the end of World War II only 20 mastiffs remained in Great Britain, but the breed was rescued by re-importing mastiffs from the U.S.A.

Neapolitan Mastiff

Present in Campania in central Italy since ancient times, the Neapolitan mastiff is Italy's contribution to the mastiff group. Although a little smaller than the English mastiff, the Neapolitan has the required broad muzzle, the heavy dewlaps, the desired height and weight, which distinguish the type. The Neapolitan mastiff is most likely descended from the Roman war and fighting 'circus' or arena dogs, which originated in Asia Minor and were

Other Names: **Mastino Napoletano**
Date of Origin: **Antiquity**
Place of Origin: **Italy**
Original Use: **Fighting, guarding livestock and property**
Modern Use: **Security, companion**
Size: Height: **26–29 in.**
       Weight: **110–150 lb**
Colors: **Black, blue, brown, gray, black-brindle, red-brindle**
Recognized by: **A.K.C., K.C.**

transported across the then known world by armies and by traders.

The Neapolitan's coat is short and fine and, on the massive head where the skin is particularly abundant and supple, it has been described as looking like 'baggy velvet'! Like the English mastiff, at the end of World War II, numbers of the Neapolitan mastiff fell dramatically. Thanks to the work of breeder Piero Scanziani, the Neapolitan mastiff was saved from extinction. Once again their sheer size does not make them the first choice as domestic pets, but they are used today in Campania as security/guard dogs and still wear their traditional broad, heavily studded, badger hair fringed collars.

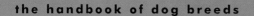

Tibetan Mastiff

Other Names: **Do-khyi**
Date of Origin: **Antiquity**
Place of Origin: **Tibet**
Original Use: **Livestock guarding**
Modern Use: **Guarding, companion**
Size: Height : **24–28 in.**
      Weight: **140–180 lb**
Colors: **Black, gray, brown, black-tan, gold**
Recognized by: **A.K.C., K.C.**

Aristotle is said to have described the Tibetan mastiff as a 'cross between a dog and a tiger', while Marco Polo wrote that they were 'as big as asses'. Either the Tibetan mastiffs they encountered were really enormous or these writers seem prone to a little exaggeration! Nevertheless the Tibetan mastiff is an impressive dog: large boned, with a broad and massive head and standing 28 in. high. Robert Leighton, in 1907, wrote in *The New Book of the Dog,* that a Tibetan mastiff called Bhotian who was being brought to England by a Major Dougall, needed an entire carriage to himself on the rail journey through India, and every time the train stopped, and Bhotian was exercised on the station platforms, he cleared them of all people!

The 'parent breed' of most of the large mountain, livestock and 'fighting dogs' of Europe, the Americas and Japan, they were used originally to guard livestock in Tibet and the Himalayas. The Tibetan mastiff came close to extinction in the late 19th century, when it was rescued by British breeders. Still rare outside the show ring, the Tibetan mastiff appears aloof, but they still retain the natural suspicion of strangers and will defend their homes and territory.

Dogue de Bordeaux

Other Names: **French mastiff**
Date of Origin: **Antiquity**
Place of Origin: **France**
Original Use: **Game hunting, guarding**
Modern Use: **Guarding, companion**
Size: Height: **23–27 in.**
          Weight: **80–100 lb**
Colors: **Mahogany, golden fawn**
Recognized by: **K.C.**

For several centuries, the Bordeaux region of France was ruled by English kings: the 'Franglais' name of *dogue* rather than *chien* is testament to this history. It appears that large dogs, native to the region, were crossed with English mastiffs (see page 212) and brought to France by the English court, together with similarly large dogs from Spain, such as the mastin Espagnol (Spanish mastiff) in order to create this large, powerful breed used originally for boar and bear hunting in southern France. Its size and fearlessness naturally attracted the attention of the 'sporting' set who used it in organized animal-baiting and in dog fighting.

The dogue de Bordeaux, with its huge head and furrows of wrinkles, looks very similar to the more recently developed bull mastiff – the product of 60% English mastiff and 40% bulldog root stock. Although the dogue de Bordeaux came briefly to a wider public knowledge in 1989, when one starred with Tom Hanks in the movie *Turner and Hooch*, the breed is still largely unknown outside France and the show rings.

Great Dane

Other Names: German mastiff, Deutsche dogge, German boarhound
Date of Origin: Middle Ages
Place of Origin: Germany
Original Use: War dog, large mammal hunting
Modern Use: Guarding, companion
Size: Height: 28–30 in.
 Weight: 100–120 lb
Colors: Black, blue, fawn, brindle, harlequin (white with black or blue patches)
Recognized by: A.K.C., K.C.

In spite of its name, the Great Dane has no connection with Denmark. It is the national dog of Germany, where it is referred to as the German mastiff or the German dog. The Great Dane can trace its ancestors back to the dogs brought to Europe by the Scythian tribe called the Alans, from the region known as Asian Russia. During the Middle Ages, the German nobility used this giant breed to hunt boar, where size, endurance, and courage were more important than looks. Nevertheless, the undisputed elegance of the Great Dane suggests that the earlier mastiffs were at some stage crossed with greyhounds (see page 96). In the 19th century in Britain, Great Danes could be found escorting the carriages of the wealthy and fashionable:

Sydenham Edwards wrote in *Cynographia Britannica* in 1800 that 'no equipage can have arrived at its acme of grandeur until a couple of harlequin Danes preceded the pomp'. Harlequin, one of the recognized colors of the breed, is a pure white underground with black or blue patches that have the appearance of being torn at the edges.

As with many large dogs with a ferocious history, the Great Dane is so confident in its abilities that it need never pick a fight: they combine elegance with power, grandeur with a good nature, and courage with docility. The sheer size of the noble Great Dane unfortunately attracts more admirers than owners and, as a breed, they suffer a high incidence of arthritis.

Boxer

Other Names: **None**
Date of Origin: **19th century**
Place of Origin: **Germany**
Original Use: **Guarding, bull baiting**
Modern Use: **Police and customs dogs, companions**
Size: Height: **21–25 in.**
Weight: **55–70 lb**
Colors: **Fawn, brindle**
Recognized by: **A.K.C., K.C.**

The boxer is one of many breeds which claims the English bulldog (see page 180) among its ancestors. But despite this, and the British-sounding name, the boxer in fact, hails from Germany. Its exact origins are uncertain, but it is thought to have descended from the *Bullenbeisser,* an ancient mastiff breed once used for boar and bull baiting. Only in the later part of the 19th century did it received a boost from bulldog bloodlines, in order to produce dogs suitable for policing German borders.

The result was a hardy, alert, strong, powerful dog with an intimidating appearance. But, at the same time, the boxer also has wonderfully expressive face – an expressiveness enhanced by its tendency to make 'questioning' noises and turn its head to one side – and a great sense of fun. Although not widely known outside Germany until after World War II, returning servicemen were full of enthusiasm for this delightful breed and, within a few years, the boxer became one of the most popular dogs in Britain and America. Still used by many police forces across Europe, the boxer is more likely, though, to be found in the home, where it makes an ideal companion dog for active families.

217

Bernese Mountain Dog

Other Names: Berner Sennenhund, Bernese cattle dog
Date of Origin: Antiquity, developed further in
    20th century
Place of Origin: Switzerland
Original Use: Drafting small carts
Modern Use: Livestock guarding, companion
Size: Height: 23–27½ in.
    Weight: 87–90 lb
Colors: Black, with rich tan and white markings
Recognized by: A.K.C., K.C.

The Bernese mountain dog is the most well known of the four Swiss mountain dogs which were split into separate breeds at the end of the 19th century. It is also the largest of the four breeds. Legend says that large, long-haired 'mastiff'-type dogs (although the term mastiff was used to refer to any big dog) were taken to Switzerland by the Roman legions, who needed large, weather-resistant dogs to guard their depots in the Alps. The descendants of these dogs stayed on and took up new roles as guards and as draft animals, pulling small carts to market for the weavers in the canton of Berne.

By the late 19th century, the Bernese had almost disappeared, overshadowed by the more glamorous Saint Bernard (see page 219). Researching the history of Swiss mountain dogs and searching the country for specimens, Franz Schertenleib located a few Bernese still in the region. Collecting the best specimens, he began a breeding program and formed a breed club to popularize them. The Bernese mountain dog was saved and became firmly established in its native land and officially named in 1908. As the breed standard stresses that the Bernese should be good natured, self-confident, and friendly, it is no surprise that this large but lovely dog has become increasingly popular in continental Europe, Britain, and in North America.

Saint Bernard

Other Names: **Alpine mastiff**
Date of Origin: **Middle Ages**
Place of Origin: **Switzerland**
Original Use: **Hauling/drafting, companion**
Modern Use: **Companion**
Size: Height: **24–28 in.**
     Weight: **110–200 lb**
Colors: **Brown-brindle, red-brindle, orange**
Recognized by: **A.K.C., K.C.**

Whether the legendary Saint Bernard ever actually rescued snow-covered travellers and offered them a reviving tot of brandy from the mythical barrel around its neck is debatable! But, like all legends, there is a kernel of truth in the story of the Saint Bernard. Descended from the great mastiff dogs brought to Switzerland by the Roman legions as guard dogs, the once-fierce dog became associated with the Hospice du Grand Saint Bernard – one of the highest human habitations in Europe and one of the oldest, for the hospice is built on the site of a Roman temple dedicated to Jupiter.

After centuries of neglect and decay, Saint Bernard of Montjoux (c.996–1081) rebuilt the mountain refuge as a place for weary pilgrims to rest. But it was not until 1707 that there is any record of dogs working at the hospice. The Saint Bernard was not an alpine 'sniffer dog' who looked for and rescued people. Instead, they acted as guide dogs and 'trail breakers', marking safe paths through snowy mountain passes.

These Saint Bernards – or Alpine mastiffs as they were then called until 1865 – were invariably smooth-haired and, while large, were more active and less weighty than today's dogs. In the 1830s, however, the breed was close to extinction but was saved by introducing Newfoundland (see page 229) bloodlines. A legacy of this crossing is to be seen in the rough-coated variety of the breed.

Estrela Mountain Dog

One of the most popular, and one of the oldest, Portuguese breeds, the Estrela, is a descendant of the Asiatic mastiffs brought to the west and used by the Romans as guard dogs. When the Romans left, the Estrela stayed in the rugged Serra da Estrela where, for centuries, it guarded flocks of livestock from wolves. Like many of the mastiff-type dogs from continental Europe, the Estrela developed to suit the location in which it lived and worked: a mountain dog, it required a dense, double coat to insulate it from winter snows and to protect it from marauding wolves. In the early 20th century, crosses with German shepherds took place, but today, thanks to the efforts of breeders in Portugal and overseas – especially in Britain – the Estrela mountain dog was returned to its pure form. The Estrela can still

Other Names: Cao da Serra da Estrela, Portuguese sheepdog
Date of Origin: Middle Ages
Place of Origin: Portugal
Original Use: Livestock guarding
Modern Use: Livestock guarding, companion
Size: Height: 24 ½– 28 ½ in.
      Weight: 66–110 lb
Colors: Black-brindle, red-brindle, fawn
Recognized by: K.C.

be found today in the mountains of Portugal guarding flocks, while herding is left to breeds such as the cao de castro laboreiro (Portuguese cattle dog) and the cao da serra de aires (Portuguese shepherd dog).

Rottweiler

Other Names: **Rottweiler Metzerhund (butcher's dog of Rottweil), 'Rotti'**

Date of Origin: **Antiquity, modern version bred in 19th century**

Place of Origin: **Germany**

Original Use: **Cattle droving, guarding**

Modern Use: **Police/military service dog, companion**

Size: Height: **23–27 in.**

Weight: **90–110 lb**

Colors: **Black with tan/mahogany markings**

Recognized by: **A.K.C., K.C.**

An ancient breed, the ancestors of the modern Rottweiler may have come to Germany with the Roman legions. As the Romans planned their assaults on foreign territories, they understood that their armies 'marched on their stomachs' but without modern refrigeration, the only way to supply fresh meat was to have it 'on the hoof'. Mass movements of cattle required strong working dogs, that were capable of both herding and guarding. One of the major supply routes led over the Alps and through the St. Gothard Pass: all along the ancient paths that led down from the pass can be found descendants of the Romans' dogs. Some of these dogs travelled further south than the Alps into southern Germany,

along the old military road through Württemberg and on to the small market town of Rottweil.

Later this region was to become an important cattle area and the Rottweiler Metzerhund – the butcher's dog of Rottweil – were said to carry the money of merchants in bags fastened around their necks since no robber would be so foolish as to challenge such a powerful and ferocious-looking dog! As the cattle market declined, however, so did the Rotti's fortune: in 1900 the town of Rottweil itself had only one dog to represent the breed. In 1912 the breed was effectively saved from extinction when it joined the police and military services and, since then, it has grown in popularity as both a working guard dog and, because it is an easier breed to obedience-train, as a family pet.

German Shepherd

Other Names: Deutscher Schäferhund, Alsatian
Date of Origin: 19th century
Place of Origin: Germany
Original Use: Sheep herding
Modern Use: Guarding/security dogs, 'assistance' dogs for the disabled, and in search & rescue in avalanches/earthquakes, companions
Size: Height: 22–26 in.
       Weight: 75–95 lb
Colors: Variety (black-tan, black-gray, solid black accepted for exhibition; cream, yellow, and long coats not widely accepted; white accepted in some countries)
Recognized by: A.K.C., K.C.

The German shepherd is quite possibly the most popular breed in the world. While 'wolf-like' dogs have existed for thousands of years and may well be the ancestors of this and other shepherding dogs like the Dutch and Belgian varieties, the 'modern' German shepherd has much more recent origins. At the end of the 19th century, Max von Stephanitz began a breeding program using a variety of sheepdogs – long-, short-, and wire-haired – from the areas of Württemberg, Thuringia, and Bavaria to produce a strong, agile shepherding dog. The resulting German shepherd was not only watchful, intelligent, responsive, energetic, and obedient, it was also very handsome.

The breed was unknown outside Germany before World War I, during which German shepherds were trained as messengers crossing shell-torn battle fields, as medical couriers carrying drugs and bandages, as search dogs locating wounded soldiers, and as guard dogs.

When hostilities ceased, a number were taken to Britain, where, perhaps to 'disassociate' the breed with Germany, they were known as Alsatians. Indiscriminate breeding in the 1920s led to problems with temperament, and incidents involving the dogs were widely reported in the press. The combination of irresponsible breeding and 'media panic' nearly destroyed the German shepherd and its numbers declined severely until they recovered their former popularity in the 1960s. Until 1915 both long-haired and wire-haired varieties were shown, but today, for show purposes, only the shortcoat is recognized.

Hovawort

Other Names: Hofwarth
Date of Origin: Middle Ages, developed in 19th century
Place of Origin: Germany
Original Use: Livestock guarding
Modern Use: Guarding, companion
Size: Height: 23–28 in.
　　　　Weight: 55–90 lb
Colors: Variety
Recognized by: K.C.

Still largely unknown outside its native Germany, the hovawart was first mentioned in 1220 as the 'hofwarth', an estate guard dog, in Eike von Repgow's *Sachsenspiegel* and, later, in the 15th century, it was recorded in Germany as a breed of dogs used to track robbers and fugitives from the law. The modern hovawart was developed by German breeders in the late 19th century in an attempt to recreate the 'great estate' dogs of the Middle Ages and Renaissance. Breeders selected a variety of 'farm dogs' from the Black Forest and Hartz mountain regions and introduced

German shepherd (see page 223), Newfoundland (see page 229), and Hungarian kuvasz (a handsome white guard dog introduced to Hungary by the Kuman, nomadic Turkish shepherds). The hovawart was first recognized in 1936 and is described as an 'elegant worker'. It is, indeed, an attractive dog and especially distinctive are the forelegs which are fringed with hair at the back of the legs and the well-feathered tail. Any breed that is both attractive and, like the hovawart, that responds well to obedience-training, gets on well with other dogs – and children – is set to become much more widely known in the future as a favored family dog.

224

Leonberger

In 1855 Heinrich Essig of Leonberg, Germany, tried to produce a dog to look like the lions on the coat of arms of the town in which he lived. As a breeder of Saint Bernards (see page 219) and Newfoundlands (see page 229), Essig crossed these along with the Landseer (the 'black-and-white Newfoundlands which were named after the artist Sir Edwin Landseer) and the Pyrenean mountain dog (see page 228) to produce the 'gentle giant' that is the Leonberger. It is possible that Essig also used a 'secret ingredient' breed, since the desired color in the Leonberger is a golden yellow – like a lion – with a black mask on the face. Establishing breed type was very difficult: when the Leonberger was first exhibited it was dismissed as a mere crossbreed, and it was not until 1949 that an official standard was published by the F.C.I. Until the late 1970s, the Leonberger was a fairly localized breed and not widely known

Other Names: **None**
Date of Origin: **19th century**
Place of Origin: **Germany**
Original Use: **Companion**
Modern Use: **Companion**
Size: Height: **26–31½ in.**
    Weight: **75–110 lb**
Colors: **Red-brown, yellow-gold**
Recognized by: **K.C.**

outside Germany, but has since made 'leaps and bounds' in Britain and the U.S.A. Its Newfoundland ancestry has not only helped to produce a very handsome breed, but one which adores swimming and, to help it along, the breed's large, round feet have webbed toes.

225

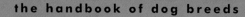

Belgian Shepherd Dog

Other Names: Chien de Berger Belge

Date of Origin: Middle Ages, developed in 19th century

Place of Origin: Belgium

Original Use: Livestock herding

Modern Use: Security/watch/guard dog (groenendael, laekenois, terveuren, Malinois), assistance dog (Malinois, tervueren)

Size: Height: 22–26 in.
      Weight: 61–63 lb

Colors and Coats: Groenendael: black, smooth.

Laekenois: Fawn, rough.

Malinois: Red, fawn, gray, smooth.

Tervueren: Red, fawn, gray; hairs are double pigmented black-tipped, long, smooth coat.

Recognized by: A.K.C., K.C. (four breeds)

Four varieties of Belgian shepherd dog exist, differing only in coat and color. Classifying Belgian shepherds is a difficult task as national kennel clubs cannot agree on naming them: in the U.S.A, the groenendael is the Belgian shepherd, while the Malinois, and the tervueren are recognized separately – but the laekenois is not recognized at all. In Britain, the Kennel Club recognizes all four breeds as distinct.

They are lightly built dogs with slender legs. The ears are erect and the tail is carried low, and all have a distinctive, high head carriage.

At the end of the 19th century, breeders all over Europe began to take a deep interest in 'native' sheepdogs and, in order to preserve these often ancient breeds, standards were set to stabilize them into as few breeds as possible. At first Belgium recognized eight standards, which included

the groenendael, a breed that was developed and refined by Belgian breeder Nicholas Rose. The groenendael is recognized by its long, smooth, black hair which is particularly abundant around the shoulders, neck and chest, well-feathered tail, and long feathering on the forelegs which extends from the forearms to the wrists.

The tervueren also has a long, straight, and abundant coat, but the colors include all shades of red, fawn, and gray. The coat is double-pigmented: the tip of each light-colored hair is colored black. The mature tervueren has a shaded coat which may be especially dark on the shoulders and back. The facial mask is also black. The tervueren descends from stock created by the groenendael: groenendael matings can sometimes produce tervueren offspring. This particular Belgian shepherd dog, which was nearly extinct by the end of World War II, is

now favored as a police and security dog. Its speciality is as a scent detector, sniffing out drugs and explosives. Its willingness to learn has also led the tervueren to be used as an assistance dog for blind and disabled owners.

The Malinois was the first Belgian shepherd dog to establish type, and it became the 'gauge' by which others were to be judged. Named after the area of Malines in Belgium, where this dog was most numerous, the Malinois has a smooth coat and in truth, resembles the German shepherd (see page 223) quite closely. Being eclipsed in popularity by the German shepherd means that the Malinois is still quite a rare breed, although, increasingly, it is being used for police and security work.

The Laekenois is the rarest of the four Belgian Shepherd Dogs: often described as a 'fawn-colored, untidy, rough, shaggy coated' dog. This description does not really do the Laekenois any justice: it is a very handsome breed with very attractive dark eyes and the hint of a moustache. Of the four Belgian shepherd dogs, only the Laekenois was a favorite of Queen Henrietta of Belgium: the breed in fact takes it name from the Chateau de Laeken, one of the queen's country residences.

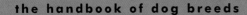

Great Pyrenees

Other Names: Chien de Montagne des Pyrenees, Great Pyrenees
Date of Origin: Antiquity
Place of Origin: France
Original Use: Sheep guarding
Modern Use: Guarding, companion
Size: Height: 26–32 in.
Weight: 45–60 kg (99–132 lb)
Colors: White, with/without patches of lemon, badger, or gray
Recognized by: A.K.C., K.C.

The Pyrenean Mountain Dog, as the breed in known in Britain, is one of the large, white 'mastiff' dogs bred in Europe centuries ago to guard herds and flocks of animals at up to 5,000 ft above sea level. The Pyrenean is probably related to the Italian maremma (see page 241), the Hungarian kuvasz ,and Turkish karabash, and is to be found on both the French and Spanish sides of the Pyrenean mountains. Because of the nature of the terrain in which it lived and worked, the Pyrenean developed its double coat with a woolly undercoat and coarse, thick, straightish outer 'jacket'. These dogs never went under cover so needed the same protection from the weather that the sheep they guarded received from their fleeces.

The Great Pyrenees dogs never herded sheep: this was left to the smaller Pyrenean sheepdogs who worked in pairs, or, to the Pyrenean mastiffs who worked in teams of four or five, herding flocks of up to 1,000 sheep. The Great Pyrenees's role was to guard the flocks against wolf attacks. To protect the dogs throats from the wolves' jaws, they traditionally wore a 'carlanca' – a spiked, iron collar. By the 18th century, some Pyreneans had come down from their mountain homes to work as guard dogs on chateaux: the Chateau at Lourdes is said to have sentry boxes large enough to accommodate the sentry and his dog. Madame de Maintenon, who saw the dogs at Barrèges in southwest France, was so impressed that she took several back to Paris and the French royal court.

Newfoundland

Many say the webbed-toed Newfoundland is a native North American breed descended from the now extinct Greater St. John's Dog; some say Lief Ericson took a black 'bear dog' named Oolum to Newfoundland in the year 1000 AD, others that Biscay fishermen brought big mountain dogs with them to the French settlements on the Newfoundland coast in Canada in 1662 to help them in their war against the British and, for this reason, some canine authorities believe that one of the Newfoundland's ancestors was the Pyrenean mountain dog (see page 228). Whatever its origins, the Newfoundland is one of the most attractive and friendly of all breeds.

Its love of swimming is well known, and the Newfoundland is famous for its impressive record for rescuing people from the water – often regardless of whether the swimmer needs or desires to be saved! The Newfoundland derives its name from the Canadian island where it worked pulling cod fishermen's nets – and

Other Names: **None**
Date of Origin: **18th century**
Place of Origin: **Canada**
Original Use: **Fisherman's assistant**
Modern Use: **Rescue dog, companion**
Size: Height: **26–28 in.**
 Weight: **110–150 lb when dry!**
Colors: **Black, brown**
Recognized by: **A.K.C., K.C.**

their boats – onto the shores. On land they were used to pull loads of firewood cut from the forests of the interior. Today, in France, Newfoundlands are used to assist the emergency services with inshore and offshore rescues.

Border Collie

Other Names: None but working dogs are often known as working collies or farm collies to distinguish them from show dogs and pets

Date of Origin: 18th century

Place of Origin: Great Britain

Original Use: Sheep/cattle herding

Modern Use: Sheep herding, sheep dog trials, companion

Size: Height: 18–21 in.

Weight: 30–49 lb

Colors: Black, black-white, brown, tricolor, blue-merle, red

Recognized by: A.K.C., K.C.

One of the world's finest and best-known sheepdogs, the Border collie takes its name from the border lands between England and Scotland. Nimble, black-and-white farms dogs bred purely for work have been portrayed since the 11th century in Britain, and it is likely that they existed long before that time. The first sheepdog trial held in Britain in Bala, Wales, in 1873 enabled shepherds to test their – and their dogs' – skills at working sheep, and the first winner was a dog form the Borders. At subsequent trials, similar dogs from the region were among the winners and so, what had previously been called a 'sheepdog' was to be called a Border collie.

Working Border collies are bred for working abilities rather than type, so only those dogs that have proven themselves to be intelligent and trainable are used for breeding. In most countries, working Border collies are registered in their own stud books rather than in national clubs, governing show dogs or other types of field trials. Owners of working dogs are generally able trace the ancestors of their dogs back through several generations and the litters from exceptional workers or champions are eagerly awaited and much sought after. Working Border collies do generally conform to type: they are black, gray or blue-merle (blue and gray mixed with black) with white points, or black, white and tan. Working Border collies are famous for their 'strong eye', which allows them to 'hold' a sheep with their gaze.

Rough Collie

Internationally famous as a the star of numerous Lassie movies (although Lassie was in fact a 'laddie'), the rough collie of today is a much more uniform – and 'prettier' dog than the functional, hard-working animal of 100 hundred years ago in the far north of Scotland. Sheep in Scotland at that time were usually dark-colored animals, and were called 'colleys', from the Anglo-Saxon word 'col' meaning black. The dogs that worked them had no breed names, but were frequently called the 'colley dogs'. These colley dogs worked for centuries, but remained largely unknown outside their working regions. When Queen Victoria made her first visit to

Other Names: Scottish collie, 'Lassie'
Date of Origin: 19th century
Place of Origin: Scotland
Original Use: Sheep herding
Modern Use: Companion
Size: Height: 20–24 in.
    Weight: 40–66 lb
Colors: Sable–white, blue-merle, tricolor
Recognized by: A.K.C., K.C.

Balmoral in Scotland in 1860, however, it was 'love at first sight' and she had a number installed at the Royal Kennels at Windsor Castle. With such patronage it was not long before the rough and ready colley dog, which was shorter in the leg and the nose than today's breed, was the object of interest among breeders.

The rough collie was one of the first breeds to be 'smartened up' for the show ring and, as appearance became the main criteria, much of the drive, energy, stamina and keenness of the working dog was lost. The once-weatherproof, truly 'rough' coat became longer, more abundant and more magnificent, but required daily grooming to prevent it matting.

Smooth Collie

The smooth collie is the only collie breed without a long coat: it's Lassie without the locks! In every respect except coat, the smooth collie conforms to the same breed standards as the rough collie (see page 231), so it's quite possible that if MGM had chosen a smooth collie to play Lassie in their movies, this breed would be much better known: outside Britain, the breed is quite rare. A widely held theory is that the rough collies worked the sheep on the hillsides, while the smooth collies were drovers, taking the sheep along the lanes and highways to market. This theory suggests that these were two different breeds but, for most of its history, the smooth collie was classified with the rough, largely because it was not unknown for smooth collies to appear in the litters of roughs.

The smooth collie breed foundation dog is generally accepted as a tricolored puppy called Trefoil, born in 1873. Although overshadowed by its more glamorous relative, the smooth collie is still an immensely attractive breed – it has all the advantages

Other Names: **None**
Date of Origin: **19th century**
Place of Origin: **Scotland**
Original Use: **Sheep herding**
Modern Use: **Companion**
Size: Height: **20–24 in.**
          Weight: **40–66 lb**
Colors: **Tricolor, blue-merle, sable-white**
Recognized by: **A.K.C., K.C.**

of the rough collie: intelligent and suited to family and urban life, good looks – including the very expressive ears which, when the dog is alert, are semi-erect but with the tips hanging over – without the disadvantages of intensive grooming!

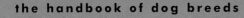

Bearded Collie

Other Names: **Highland collie, beardie**
Date of Origin: **16th century**
Place of Origin: **Great Britain**
Original Use: **Sheep droving**
Modern Use: **Companion**
Size: Height: **51–56 cm (20–22 in)**
Weight: **18–27 kg (40–60 lb)**
Colors: **Black, brown, blue, fawn, gray**
Recognized by: **A.K.C., K.C.**

'Shaggy sheepdogs' like the bearded collie appear to have been hard at work herding sheep in Scotland for centuries, but this breed was only officially recognized in Britain in 1944! One theory is that the Highland collie as it was long called, is related to the komondor – the gloriously 'dread–locked' sheepdog from Hungary – which, hundreds of years ago, was taken by the Magyars to Poland, and thence to Scotland: the Poles sent grain (and komondors) and, in return, received Scottish sheep. By this theory, it is also possible that the beardie has Polish lowland sheepdog in its genetic make up: in looks the beardie is closer to this breed than the corded–coated komondor. Until the early 20th century the breed was largely unknown outside of Scotland, where it could be found working as a drover rather than a herding dog.

While a breed club was formed in 1912, the beardie did not make a significant impact on the public and, by the end of World War II, the beardie had almost disappeared as a working dog. The breed was rescued from extinction by a Mrs. Willison, who had acquired a beardie by accident: she was looking for a Shetland sheepdog (see page 235) bred from working parents, but the farmer from whom she had ordered it sent her an 'odd' puppy instead. It took some time to work out what breed the dog was, but Jeannie as the puppy was called (later Champion Jeannie of Bothkennar) was mated with Baillie – another beardie who was fortunately spotted by Mrs. Willison playing happily on Brighton Beach, in Sussex, and these two revived the breed.

Shetland Sheepdog

Other Names: **Dwarf Scottish shepherd, Sheltie**
Date of Origin: **18th century**
Place of Origin: **Shetland Islands, Scotland**
Original Use: **Sheep/pony herding**
Modern Use: **Sheep herding, companion**
Size: Height: **14–15 in.**
　　　Weight: **14–16 lb**
Colors: **Black–tan, black–white, blue–merle,**
　　　sable, tricolor
Recognized by: **A.K.C., K.C.**

At first glance, the Sheltie looks like a miniature rough collie (see page 231) and this has led many to believe that the Sheltie was a deliberate bantamisation of the larger dog. This is not the case, as all the domesticated animals of the Shetland Islands – the famous Shetland ponies are the best–known examples, but the sheep and cattle too – tend to be dwarfed compared to their mainland counterparts. This is in part due to the subsistence level of life in the islands which favored smaller animals and, with an isolated population, inbreeding occurs which also tended to encourage small size. It may well be that the Sheltie descends then from small, rough collies imported to the islands on account of their already suitable size.

Like the rough collie, the Sheltie of 100 years ago was far plainer and, perhaps rougher, in appearance than today's dogs. Few descriptions exist of the dogs except to say that they were often 'speckled' and 'foxy–faced': working ability was more valuable than looks. As well as herding, the Shelties were also used to stop sheep from grazing on the valuable vegetables grown in gardens by the islanders. The modern, very beautiful, Sheltie is of recent origin, for they were only recognized by the Kennel Club in 1909 and, since that time, improvements in the looks of the breed have been made, especially to produce the profuse coat with its abundant frill and mane. An exceptionally gentle and sweet–natured breed, while rarely used today as a working dog, the Sheltie still retains many of its guarding and herding instincts.

Old English Sheepdog

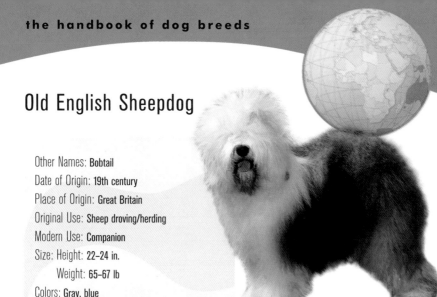

Other Names: **Bobtail**
Date of Origin: **19th century**
Place of Origin: **Great Britain**
Original Use: **Sheep droving/herding**
Modern Use: **Companion**
Size: Height: **22–24 in.**
        Weight: **65–67 lb**
Colors: **Gray, blue**
Recognized by: **A.K.C., K.C.**

One of the family of 'shaggy sheepdogs' that spread across Europe – from the south in Italy to the north in Russia, to the east in Hungary and west to Britain – the Old English sheepdog, in spite of its name, is probably only about 200 years old. It is probably a descendant of the bearded collie (see page 234) and foreign breeds such as the briard (see page 239): until a system of registration of pedigrees was introduced in 1873, matings, especially in working breeds, were more indiscriminate than today. Owners who wanted their working dogs to perform specific jobs were more concerned with propagating dogs with the desired working qualities rather than preserving a particular type. For sheep farmers in England's West Country, intelligence, stamina, hardiness, and agility were what a dog required, and these could

be found in the 'bobtail' as the breed was also called. It earned this name because drover dogs – those that drove the herds to markets – were exempted from taxes and tolls along the road to markets. To prove they were drovers, their tails were docked. The popular belief that the Old English is a tailless breed is false: the majority of puppies are born with tails that require docking.

Selective breeding, which began in the 1880s, has altered the Old English somewhat: it is now a much bigger and heavier dog than it was originally, the coat has become longer, more profuse and much softer in texture. Once, grooming would have been difficult, today it's a Herculean task! Nevertheless, the Old English retains its loud and resonant bark and its deceptively slow, ambling gait – until it turns into a gallop.

Australian Shepherd Dog

Although its ancestors include sheepdogs from Australia and New Zealand, the Australian shepherd dog was 'born' in the United States of America in the 19th century, where is was bred as a working shepherd dog that was suitable for the varied climate of California. Since then, the breed has gone on to distinguish itself in a whole range of fields including search and rescue. Its affectionate and playful yet calm temperament – likened to golden and Labrador retrievers (see pages 70 and 74) – has ensured it a place in many hearts and homes.

Currently, the Australian shepherd dog is little known outside the United States, except for in the show ring, and some breeders are working towards reducing the size of the dog, which would further increase its popularity as a pet. It is already a good-looking dog with a delightful coat, a predominantly brown nose, sparkling eyes and very attractive, well-feathered hind legs. In time, the Australian shepherd dog will become a firm favorite with dog lovers the world over.

Other Names: **None**
Date of Origin: **20th century**
Place of Origin: **United States of America**
Original Use: **Sheep herding**
Modern Use: **Sheep herding, service/search and rescue, companion**
Size: Height: **18–23 in.**
 Weight: **35–70 lb**
Colors: **Black, blue-merle, liver, red**
Recognized by: **A.K.C., K.C.**

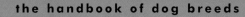

Australian Cattle Dog

Other Names: Hall's heeler, blue heeler,
Queensland heeler, Australian heeler
Date of Origin: 19th century
Place of Origin: Australia
Original Use: Cattle herding
Modern Use: Cattle herding, companion
Size: Height: 17–20 in.
Weight: 35–45 lb
Colors: Blue, red
Recognized by: A.K.C., K.C.

Australia has developed two of the finest working dogs that ever worked in the service of man: the kelpie and the Australian cattle dog, which predates the former by some 30 years. The first working cattle dogs in Australia, were the now-extinct 'black bobtails', but these were big, clumsy dogs that were unsuited to both the intense heat and great distances involved in driving cattle in Australia.

Thomas Smith Hall needed a dog to round up, drive and pen range cattle – which are pretty wild animals – so any dog needed to be rugged, agile, intelligent, and capable of delivering a bite to the heel of a bull without crippling it or damaging the hide.

Such dogs were generally called 'heelers' and would test the range and speed of cattle by feinting. They snap or bite the heel of the leg bearing the steer's weight. However, a well-aimed kick from a steer is fast and potentially lethal so, after the bite, the heeler drops flat to the ground so it is under the kick. Hall also wanted to exploit the native dingo's ability to sneak silently up on its prey. 'Hall's heeler', as the breed was once called is the result of crosses with dingoes, the now extinct Smithfield, kelpies, blue-merle smooth collies (see page 223), bull terriers and, Dalmatians (see page 183). Like 'dallies' Australian cattle dog puppies are born white (or white with black speckles) regardless of their later color and, like dingoes, they are wary by nature and need early socialisation with both people and other dogs.

Briard

Other Names: Berger de Brie
Date of Origin: Middle Ages, developed in 19th century
Place of Origin: France
Original Use: Livestock guarding/herding
Modern Use: Security/guard dog, companion
Size: Height: 23–27 in.
        Weight: 74–76 lb
Colors: Black, fawn
Recognized by: A.K.C., K.C.

Although its exact origins are unknown, the briard, which takes its name from the French province of Brie (most famous for its cheese), is most likely to be a member of the ancient race of sheepdogs that came to Europe from Asia in the company of the invading hoards, which swept across the continent from late Roman times through the early Middle Ages. Other dogs which belong to this group are the Hungarian komondor, kuvasz, and the puli (see page 244) the bearded collie (see page 234) and the Old English sheepdog (see page 236). While these breeds differ in many respects, they are all roughly similar in both conformation and in the work they were bred to carry out. The briard was once classified as the 'goat-haired' variety of the beauceron: this dog is also from Brie, and shares the same double dew claws and the hind feet.

Once used as a herding and watchdog, the briard distinguished itself in World War I in the service of the French army. Wearing specially made backpacks, the briard carried ammunition and gun parts from depots to the front lines and, for the Red Cross, it carried first-aid supplies and located wounded soldiers in the battlefield. Today the briard is one of France's most popular companion dogs, and is gaining a foothold in homes in Britain and the United States of America.

Bergamasco

Other Names: **Cane de Pastore Bergamasco,**
  Bergamese shepherd
Date of Origin: **Antiquity**
Place of Origin: **Italy**
Original Use: **Livestock guarding**
Modern Use: **Guarding, companion**
Size: Height: **22–24 in.**
Weight: **57–84 lb**
Colors: **Various**
Recognized by: **K.C.**

The most distinctive feature of the Bergamasco is its soft, long hair, which forms wavy 'flocks' – though most would call them 'dreadlocks'! A breed that is at least 2,000 years old – if not more – the Bergamasco is named after the Bergamo region of northern Italy where it was used to guard livestock and where its coat developed into a weatherproof jacket that also protected the dog from the flailing hooves of large livestock and from the jaws of wolves. It is possible that the Bergamasco is related to the briard (see page 239) although its corded coat has more in common with the Hungarian komondor. Like both breeds, the Bergamasco is a highly efficient and enthusiastic worker, but is also little known, even in Italy, and the breed has come close to extinction several times in its recent history. While it is affectionate, it is a breed that is best suited to outdoors, and not to city life. Nevertheless, the breed is secure in the hands of a number of enthusiastic owners and breeders.

Maremma Sheepdog

The pure white maremma is a native of Tuscany and the Abruzzi region of Italy and is a descendant of the great, white eastern sheepdogs that spread westwards with the Magyars across Europe over 1,000 years ago, leaving their legacy in breeds such as the maremma and the Pyrenean mountain dog (see page 228). The maremma today is smaller than its older relatives, the shorter-coated maremmano sheepdog and the Abruzzese mountain dog, but retains its white color which was preferred by shepherds so that their dogs could be readily distinguished from wolves and so that the sheep the dogs guarded would accept their presence more willingly. Older maremmas show a tinge of biscuit or

Other Names: Maremma, pastore Abruzzese, central Italian sheepdog
Date of Origin: Antiquity
Place of Origin: Italy
Original Use: Flock guarding
Modern Use: Security, companion
Size: Height: 23½– 28½ in.
Weight: 66–100 lb
Colors: White
Recognized by: K.C.

lemon in their ears, and the youthful black nose becomes slightly pinkish-brown – but no less distinguished – with age. The abundant, long (except on the head) harsh coat is weatherproof, has a slight wave to it, and forms a ruff around the neck. The tail is thickly feathered, forming a magnificent plume. Like many of the flock-guarding breeds, the maremma makes an efficient guard dog, although obedience-training is not easy. The maremma has been shown regularly in Britain since 1931 but it is still rare in other countries outside Italy.

Polish Lowland Sheepdog

Other Names: **Polski owczarek nizinny**
Date of Origin: **16th century**
Place of Origin: **Poland**
Original Use: **Hunting**
Modern Use: **Herding, companion**
Size: Height: **16–20 in.**
     Weight: **30–35 lb**
Colors: **Any**
Recognized by: **A.K.C., K.C.**

The Polish lowland sheepdog is considered by many to be the 'bridge' or 'link' breed between the Asian corded-coat herding dogs brought to Europe from the east by the Magyars over 1,000 years ago and whose descendants include the Hungarian puli (see page 244) the Bergamasco (see page 240) and the komondor, and the more recent 'shaggy sheepdog' breeds such as the bearded collie (see page 234).

Numerous dogs of this type are to be found across Europe: the Catalan sheepdog in Spain, the Portuguese shepherd dog, and the schapendo (Dutch sheepdog) all bred in their native lands as working dogs. Consequently, except in show rings, breeds like the Polish lowland, are rarely seen outside their homelands, where many are still, in fact, working dogs.

Like many shepherding breeds, interest in 'indigenous' breeds started in the late 19th century — when mechanization in agriculture was taking over the roles formerly performed by animals. Without this interest, many of these breeds would have become extinct. To add to many such breed's problems, two World Wars did much to speed their decline. The Polish lowland was fortunate, however, in that enthusiastic Polish breeders in the late 1940s were able to successfully revive the breed, which is now a popular household companion in Poland.

Anatolian Shepherd Dog

The handsome Anatolian shepherd dog from central Turkey is another of the large guarding breeds used by shepherds across Europe and Asia for centuries. These dogs were not herding dogs – they were not expected to control the flocks; instead their job was to protect them, especially against wolves. The Anatolian is probably related to the mastiff, for it has the size, speed, stamina, and broad head which distinguishes this group of dogs. In Turkey, sheepdogs were collectively classified as 'coban kopegi' but in the 1970s breeders began to investigate type and found several regional differences such as the akbash dog from western Turkey. Coban Kopegi was originally the over-arching Turkish term for a number of shepherd dogs such as the Anatolian from central Turkey and the Akbash from western Turkey.

Other Names: **Coban kopegi, karabas, kangal dog, Anatolian karabash dog**
Date of Origin: **Middle Ages**
Place of Origin: **Turkey**
Original Use: **Sheep guarding**
Modern Use: **Sheep guarding**
Size: Height: **28–32 in.**
Weight: **90–140 lb**
Colors: **Variety**
Recognized by: **A.K.C., K.C.**

These are now seen as distinct breeds- although the K.C. only recognizes the Anatolian and the Akbash is not recognized by anyone except Turkish shepherds and Turkish sheep! The Anatolian's coat is dense and smooth, with a thick insulating undercoat. The most usual color is fawn – lighter colors in flock-guarding breeds were generally preferred so the dogs could be distinguished from wolves – with a black mask. A white version, and other varied colors are also recognized.

The Anatolian shepherd dog can still be found guarding flocks from wolves, which still range central Asia. Bred specifically for work, the Anatolian is not regarded as a suitable companion dog unless there is early socialization with humans and other dogs.

243

Hungarian Puli

Other Names: Juhasz kutya, puli, Hungarian water dog
Date of Origin: Middle Ages
Place of Origin: Hungary
Original Use: Sheep herding
Modern Use: Retrieving, companion
Size: Height: 14½–17½ in.
       Weight: 22–33 lb
Colors: Black, apricot, white
Recognized by: A.K.C., K.C.

From the great Hungarian sheep-grazing plains known as the Puszta, the Hungarian puli is possibly the best known of the four great Hungarian shepherding breeds. Its most distinctive feature is its coat, which in the case of show dogs, grows to floor length and falls naturally into narrow cords as the dog matures (puppies are born without cording). The overall impression is of a dog hidden by a very large string floor mop! So densely covered is the puli that it's sometimes difficult to tell which end of the dog is which!

The virtually waterproof puli with its distinctive 'dreadlocks' is almost certainly the ancestor of the poodle (see page 194) and there is even a poodle with the same corded coat. Both these breeds have been used as gun dogs, retrieving shot water fowl. In Hungary, the puli and the pumi (created by crosses between puli and softer coated German spitzen) were often classed together under the name juhasz kutya, which simply means 'shepherd's dogs'. The ancestry of the puli is uncertain, but an early mention in 1751 by a Hungarian writer called Heppe, described such a cord-coated dog, which he called the Hungarian beater dog, and claimed it was used to hunt ducks – and rabbits! Consensus today generally puts the likely contenders for the ancestor of the puli among the Asiatic dogs that came to Hungary with the Magyar invasions. World War II nearly saw the end of the puli in Hungary, but a group of expatriates were able to re-establish the breed abroad. particularly in North America, where it became a popular companion dog. Pulis – or more correctly in Hungarian, pulik, the plural of puli – have also been trained for police work in Germany.

Cardigan Welsh Corgi

Other Names: **Corgi**
Date of Origin: **Middle Ages**
Place of Origin: **Wales**
Original Use: **Cattle drover**
Modern Use: **Livestock drover, companion**
Size: Height: **10½–12½ in.**
　　　　Weight: **25–38 lb**
Colors: **Any**
Recognized by: **A.K.C., K.C.**

Corgis were – and on some Welsh farms continue to be – cattle dogs and belong to a group of dogs often called 'heelers'. Nimble, active, and very strong, these dogs have fairly long bodies and short legs and their job was to fly in and nip the heels of cattle to hurry them along. Their short stature meant they could then lie close to the ground and avoid any hooves that were kicked out. The original Celtic meaning of the name corgi is simply 'dog'. Tradition holds that, after the Norman Conquest in 1066, native Britons were prohibited from owning the 'blue-blooded' hounds of their French overlords and 'corgi' became corrupted to 'curgi' and finally to 'cur', a word still used today to refer to a mongrel or random bred dog. Others, however, contend that 'cor' means 'dwarf' and 'gi' means dog, but this word

does not make any appearance in Middle English writing until around 1360. The Cardigan and the Pembroke (see page 246) corgis both come from South Wales but each is a distinct breed in its own right. The isolated nature of the farms in the Welsh valleys meant that the two remained pure breeds.

Whether it came with the Celts over 3,000 years ago, or as other think, it is related to the short legged continental bassets that came to Britain with the Normans, the Cardigan Welsh corgi has remained relatively unchanged since it arrived in Wales: it still has its long 'fox's brush' of a tail and large, upright ears. The Cardigan is the quieter and more placid of the two corgi breeds – but it is still a very watchful and quite snappy defender of its property.

Pembroke Welsh Corgi

Other Names: **Corgi**
Date of Origin: **10th century**
Place of Origin: **Wales**
Original Use: **Cattle d rover**
Modern Use: **livestock drover, companion**
Size: Height: **10–12 in.**
 Weight: **20–26 lb**
Colors: **Black-tan, red, fawn, sable**
Recognized by: **A.K.C., K.C.**

The Pembroke Welsh corgi is the better known of the two corgi breeds – largely because these are the corgis that are often seen accompanying the British Royal family. There are two main theories regarding the origins of the Pembroke: one is that a dwarf dog was brought to England by Flemish weavers in about 1100. Some of these weavers then moved to the southwest corner of Wales. What weavers would need cattle dogs for is uncertain, except that their small size may have made them the choice for companion dogs. If the Pembroke is of Flemish origins, then it is said this corgi is a descendant of the sptiz-type dogs and is related to the schipperke (see page 196). Both the Pembroke and the schipperke have 'foxy' faces, but where did the long body, short legs and big ears come from? Furthermore, the relationship to the schipperke would not explain the Pembroke's lack of a tail!

The second, more plausible theory is that the Pembroke is, like the Cardigan, descended from the continental short-legged bassets, and that the isolation of the farms and the tendency of farmers to breed for working characteristics accounts for the differences in the two corgi breeds. Another suggestion is that the Pembroke is also related to the Swedish Vallhund (see page 211): it may be possible that, after pillaging Britain, the little heeler was taken back to Scandinavia as booty!

In the early part of the 20th century, Cardigan corgis were taken to Pembrokeshire and the two interbred, which reduced the differences between the two breeds. In 1934, the two breeds were recognized as distinct. Like the Cardigan corgi, the Pembroke corgi can still be found working, but it is more likely to be found as a companion dog – both in Wales, and across the world.

Lancashire Heeler

Recognized only as recently as 1981 in Britain, the work of the Lancashire heeler and other heeler breeds became unnecessary with advancing mechanisation and, along with the Yorkshire and Norfolk heelers, and the Smithfield collie (so called because it worked at London's Smithfield meat market) the Lancashire heeler became extinct. The modern Lancashire heeler is therefore a re-creation of the breed that took place in the 1960s and is the result of crosses between Welsh Corgis (see pages 245 and 246) – themselves heelers and providers of the Lancashire's conformation – and Manchester terriers (see page 137) who provided the smooth, glossy black coat with its rich tan markings.

The 'new breed' is almost identical to its ancient namesake, which was used in the district around Ormskirk in Lancashire, northwest England, by butchers and slaughter men to control and direct cattle.

Other Names: **Ormskirk heeler, 'nip 'n duck' dog**
Date of Origin: **17th century, re-created in 1960s**
Place of Origin: **Great Britain**
Original Use: **Cattle drover**
Modern Use: **Companion**
Size: Height: **10–12 in.**
     Weight: **6–13 lb**
Colors: **Black–tan**
Recognized by: **K.C.**

The dogs were generally called 'nip'n duck' dogs, which described perfectly their method of working. The modern breed is not used as a cattle dog, but instead displays more of its terrier ancestry in its enthusiasm for chasing rabbits and squirrels!

Doberman Pinscher

Other Names: **Doberman**
Date of Origin: **19th century**
Place of Origin: **Germany**
Original Use: **Guarding**
Modern Use: **Security/guard dog, companion**
Size: Height: **25½–27 in.**
      Weight: **66–88 lb**
Colors: **Black, brown, blue, fawn**
Recognized by: **A.K.C., K.C.**

The elegant, obedient and often very affectionate Doberman is a relatively recent and deliberately 'manufactured' breed. In the 1870s German tax collector, Louis Dobermann of Apolda, in Thuringia, Germany, began experimental breeding to produce a guard dog 'par excellence'. He used Rottweilers (see page 222), German Pinschers (see page 186), Weimaranas (see page 68), English greyhounds (see page 96) and Manchester Terriers (see page 137). By 1890, Herr Dobermann had arrived at a type which suited his requirements: a giant terrier with the strength and guarding abilities of the famed Thuringian shepherd dogs. According to early commentators on the breed, the Doberman was certainly fearless and most thought that a good deal of courage was needed to own one: legend tells of one Doberman exported to the U.S.A. that was awarded Best in Breed three times before any judge dared to open the dog's mouth. It was only then that a serious fault was discovered: the Best in Breed had missing teeth!

Following the wishes of Herr Dobermann, a later breeder, Otto Goeller added pinscher (meaning 'terrier') to the name. Today, the Doberman pinscher is perhaps the most famous, and perhaps the best, guard dog in existence and is used the world over by police and security companies. But with socialization in infancy, Dobermans have also proved themselves to be excellent companion dogs.

Glossary

Bat ear	An erect ear, broad at base and rounded at top
Bay	The prolonged sound of a hunting dog
Beard	Thick long hair on the muzzle
Blaze	White stripe running up the centre of the face
Blenheim	Chestnut and white color
Blue-merle	Marbled blue and gray, mixed with black
Bobtail	Naturally tailless dog or one with docked tail (see below)
Breed standard	Description of the breed against which dogs are judged at shows
Brindle	Mix of black hairs with brown, light gold, red, or gray hairs
Broken coat	Wire-haired coat
Button ear	An ear where the flap folds forward with the tip close to the skull
Corded coat	A coat of separate, rope-like twists of hair, formed from intertwined top and undercoat hairs
Cropping	Amputating the ears to enable the remaining part to stand erect

Crossbreed	The offspring of parents of two different breeds
Dam	Female parent
Dew claw	Fifth digit (thumb) on inside of leg
Dewlap	Loose pendulous skin under throat
Docking	Amputating the tail
Domed skull	An evenly rounded head
Double coat	Warm and waterproof undercoat and weather-resistant outer coat
Drop ear	Folded, drooping ear
Feathering	Long fringes of hair
Flews	Pendulous upper lips
Giving tongue	The barking or baying (see above) of hounds
Grizzle	Mix of colors including bluish-gray, red, and black
Hackney action	High lifting front feet
Harlequin	Patched colors of black or blue on white
Height	Distance from top of withers (see below) to the ground
Hock	The tarsal bones, forming the joint between the knee and toes
Inbreeding	Mating closely related dogs
Interbreeding	Breeding together dogs of different varieties of a breed

Line breeding	Mating of related dogs in a family or to a common ancestor
Mask	Dark shading on the fore face
Merle	Blue-gray with flecks of black
Molt	Shedding of the coat
Muzzle	The fore face, the face in front of the eyes
Occiput	The highest, upper point of the skull
Pads	Thickened cushions beneath the toes and on soles of the feet
Part-colored	Two colors in variegated patches
Pastern	The region between the wrist and the toes
Pedigree	A dog's ancestry
Pied	Unequally proportioned patches of white and another color
Plume	A long fringe of hair hanging from the tail
Pointing	Freezing on sight of game and pointing in direction of game
Pricked ears	Erect, pointed ears
Pure bred	A dog whose parent belong to the same breed
Random bred dog	A dog whose parents do not both belong to a recognized breed
Retrieve	The act of bring back game or other item to a handler

Roan	A fine mix of colored hairs alternating with white hairs
Rose ear	A small drop ear folding over and back
Runt	The weakest, often the smallest puppy in a litter
Sable	Black tipped hairs on a background of gold, silver, gray, or tan
Sabre tail	A tail carried in a curve
Scent hound	A hound that hunts by ground scent
Self color	Whole color except for lighter shading
Setting	Freezing on sight of game and flushing game on command
Sickle tail	A tail carried out and up in a semicircle
Sight hound	A hound that hunts more by sight than scent
Sire	Male parent
Stop	The depression before the eyes between the skull and the muzzle
Topknot	Longer hair on top of head
Trail	To hunt by following ground scent
Tricolor	Three colors – black, white and tan
Wheaten	Pale yellow or fawn color
Withers	The highest point on the body just behind the neck

Acknowledgements

With thanks to Vic Swift at the British
Library, London for assistance, and to all
owners, breeders, and enthusiasts who
placed details of dogs, dog breeds, and
'shaggy dog stories' on the internet.

Selected Bibliography

Dr. Bruce Fogel **The New
Encyclopaedia of the Dog** Dorling
Kindersley, 1995
Collins Gem Dogs Harper Collins, 1996
Stanley Dangerfield and Elsworth Howell
(eds.) **The International Encyclopaedia
of Dogs** Pelham Books, 1971
Kay White **The Wonderful World of
Dogs** Hamlyn, 1976

Associations

The British Kennel Club
1–5 Clarges Street,
Piccadilly,
London
W1Y 8AB
www.the–kennel–club.org.uk

Federation Cynologique Internationale (FCI)
Place Albert 1,
13 B–6530,
Thurin,
Belgium
www.fci.be

American Kennel Club
260 Madison Ave
New York
NY 10016
www.akc.org

United Kennel Club
100 East Kilgore rod
Kalamazoo
Missouri 49002–5584
www.ukcdog.com

Index